The Alchemy of Depression

The Secrets Lie Within

Tracey Terry

First published in 2023 by Tracey Terry

© Tracey, Terry
The moral rights of the author have been asserted.
This book is an Inspirational Book Writers book.

Author: Terry, Tracey
Title: The Alchemy of Depression; The Secrets Lie Within
ISBN: 9798852679543

Editor-in-chief: Keziah Daniel
Cover Design: Sarah Rose Graphic Design

Disclaimer:
The material in this publication is of the nature of general professional advice, but it is not intended to provide specific guidance for particular circumstances and it should not be relied on as the basis for any decision to take action or not take action on any particular matter which it covers. Readers should obtain individual advice from the author where appropriate, before making any such decision. To the maximum extent permitted by law, the author and publisher disclaim all responsibility and liability to any person, arising directly or indirectly from any person taking or not taking action based on the information in this publication.

We acknowledge that mental illness is a real problem and does require support and, at times, intervention and treatment. The views in this book are based on personal experience and do not override the views and diagnoses of medical professionals.

Dedication

This book is dedicated to my incredible family, who have been so patient and loving with my growth, supported me through all the ups and downs, and never given up on me no matter what I put them through.

I also dedicate this to all the people who think they are stuck. Whose lives I hope to impact for the better, that they come to realise they can transform their depression – it is possible. And that they find it is much simpler than they believed and that they can find true happiness as I have.

I am so grateful to my beautiful friend and mentor, Elizabeth Hughes, who has supported and encouraged me since day dot and has really shown me how it is possible to believe in myself and what I can achieve with that belief.

I really want to thank the amazing team at Inspirational Book Writers for coaching me through to bring this book to fruition as there were times I felt great fear in sharing. I am especially grateful to my amazing editor, Keziah Daniels who was truly inspirational in guiding me on with her feedback and prompts.

I also wish to thank the incredible women at the House of Brand Magic who have helped me to hone in on my vision for my business and how I can help others.

Let Love

"Let love overtake you.
Let love overwhelm you.
Let love ever guide you.
Let love, love, love.

For all times, eternal.
For all ways, forever.
For all paths united
In love, love, love.

May My Heart be within you.
May My Spirit flow through you.
May My Face guide you onwards
With love, blessed, love.

Let love overtake you.
Let love overwhelm you.
Let love ever guide you.
Become love.

May My Heart beat with your heart,
May our heart's blood run freely.
May all hearts join the One Heart.
In love, blessed love.

Together, forever.
Forgiven, all forgiven.
May My peace be with you
Eternally love.

Let love overtake you.
Let love overwhelm you.
Let love ever guide you.
Become love."

Lyrics Chandra Easton – http://www.starastrologyhealing.com
Music Arjuna Govinda – http://www.musicheartjourney.com

Foreward

Finally, a book that gets to the heart of natural healing for depression.

Having lost my first partner to suicide, I know the devastating effects that depression has on individuals, families, and whole communities. I have made it my life's mission to help others through psychology, kinesiology, and energy healing and to let people know they have options.

Knowing Tracey for over ten years on a professional level, as a student of my Kinesiology and Energy Reset courses, and now as a fellow author, I can wholeheartedly say that she walks the talk and always comes from a place of genuine compassion and empathy for everyone she reaches out to.

Through this brave book, Tracey openly and honestly shares her story. Her rawness and experience so well described, it will bring you to tears and then have you cheering her on as she overcomes her illness with grace and humour. She generously shares all the knowledge and wisdom she has learnt on the way.

Anyone who has suffered from depression will identify with Tracey's story and now realise that there are natural methods and so much more help available than they may have explored already. Her simple and practical suggestions make it easy for you to follow even when you are exhausted and depressed.

I am sure this book will be an inspiring source to many as Tracey highlights a multitude of ways and techniques that have helped her journey through this crippling illness. I love her concept that you can make a conscious decision to heal, set the intention and know you are worth it, and never give up. There is a light at the end of the tunnel.

May you all find ways of alchemising your depression into gold.

Elizabeth Hughes BA (Hons) Ed.Psych. ATMS
Best-selling author, teacher and founder of
Your Body Has The Answer Ltd

Acknowledgements

This amazing work is a rare and honest insight into the roller coaster journey of an amazing woman who battled depression.

I have been fortunate not to have suffered depression, and yet could still relate to so many of Tracey's feelings, stories, ups and downs and the beautiful supports that she implemented into her and her family's life to rise above this incredibly debilitating disease.

Reading this raw and honest book is like walking along a set of parallel paths. Tracey openly shares her experiences, battles and feelings along one path, whilst holding your hand and supporting you on the other, sharing so many practical, natural methods that promote healing and wellness.

Whether having experienced depression yourself, supported loved ones with depression or just having battled the many ups and downs of life, I am confident that Tracey's story will inspire you to choose healing over hurting.

Bronwyn Ziviani
Bach Ed, Bach Teach, Dip Kinesiology
A Welcome Change Holistic Healing
Highfields, Qld.

Being a naturopath of many decades, I have seen mental health explode and be at the forefront of our needs today. Tracey has written a deeply heart centered book, that gives hope and a practical path that has been lived, and can help the reader transform depression and take back control of their life

Jennifer Jefferies
The Present Day Wise Woman
http://jenniferjefferies.com/

Hi Tracey, It's been such an honour editing for you. I found your book to be immensely generous in all the love, support, and wisdom given in such a practical and useful way. I have started using many of the tools myself and have no doubt that your book is going to change lives. I also enjoyed the intuitive connection or energetic connection that is just part of it energetically. That is amazing and special! Congratulations on your beautiful book.

Sincerely,
Keziah

Table of Contents

Lifting the Veil of Depression
Believe Anything is Possible!

My Journey at its Worst

I was tired of lying on the couch, lifeless, unable to move or be bothered doing anything as a result of the numbing medication that I felt had totally dumbed me down. Was this better than endless crying? Where had my zest for life gone? I was exhausted! What was to happen to my gorgeous children and husband, who didn't deserve a zombie or else a crying, blithering mess? I wanted to feel better.

I wanted freedom from my mind, from the deep pressure I constantly and relentlessly put on myself. From constantly rejecting myself, from my total lack of self-esteem and self-love. It was time to let go. To let go of these old thoughts and beliefs that haunted me, so I could become free of the endless line of pills – of pharmaceutical meds. I desperately needed to free and find myself. I realised that the meds were just covering up what needed to be healed. My depression was trying to tell me something… I finally asked the question, "How?" "How can I heal and feel better?"

These thoughts took me on a journey to discover how to heal myself, which I did. Through what I learnt and studied along the way, I have now become a Kinesiologist, Reiki Master, Energy Alchemist, Energy Reset Practitioner, and a therapist of many other modalities. And I want to share some of what I learnt with you through this book to help start YOU on YOUR transformation.

I had lived in a state of depression up to my early 40s (I am now 57). I had tried to commit suicide in my teenage years and thought about it many times after. When I was 32, after the birth of my second child, I finally sought help from our local GP for my family's sake. I had previously been to psychologists with little result. The GP treated me for chronic fatigue and depression for a while with little success and referred me to a psychiatrist. I was clinically diagnosed with "severe depression" and "obsessive-compulsive disorder". I was put on the highest dose of antidepressants possible. I was told I would have to remain on the drug for the rest of my life (to me, it was indeed a lifetime sentence of imprisonment). I did get other opinions which confirmed this diagnosis and told me I was incurable.

I was also popping Paracetamol like lollies (which unfortunately people take far too often and which do more harm than good) as well as other meds to counteract the effects of the antidepressants, which were causing other health issues. Finally, after three years of living an over-the-counter drug-induced, unhealthy, and meaningless existence, I decided enough was enough. I was going to

escape… No, not through thoughts as I had had in the past of ending my life… Just the fact I wasn't going to live my life this way any longer. I sought "other" assistance. At that stage, despite being Catholic, I had no belief in higher beings who could really help. I wasn't sure I actually believed in God and didn't think He could help if He did exist. I didn't realise how much help was available from within and above and that I was a lot more powerful than I thought.

After deciding this would not be my fate, I started asking, "How?" "How do I get off this medicine and repair my life?" (Not really sure who I was asking!) Not only for my sake but for the sake of my gorgeous husband and two beautiful girls (3 and 4) who deserved better than this. The answers came thick and fast from inspiration and from people who were suddenly presenting me with ideas. I discovered there is so much we can do, so many alternatives available to us. I was able to stop my medication, and while it took me more years after that to finally be truly happy, it has been an amazing journey. And, I was able to conceive again, which the doctors had told me was also impossible.

Deciding Transformation IS Possible

"Alice laughed. 'There's no use trying,' she said. 'One can't believe impossible things.' 'I daresay you haven't had much practice,' said the Queen. 'When I was your age, I always did it half an hour a day. Why, sometimes, I've believed as many as six impossible things before breakfast.'"

—Lewis Carroll

I know people going through depression are looking for a way out, a way to find themselves again – as that was me. Are you sick of hearing the way you talk to yourself and others? Of being sad, angry, confused, and unable to function? Are you tired of the medical treadmill, wanting to escape the depression stigma and label? Are you totally over feeling numb, exhausted, lifeless… And finally wanting some answers, so you can take your life back? Perhaps you are being dumbed down with medication and or booze? Would you like to connect and find yourself and your reason for being here? To just live a happy life on your own terms?

Aptly termed "The Black Dog" or "The Dark Night of the Soul", I know depression can leave you feeling dark and heavy without any apparent reason. My experience may be very different from yours and indeed someone else's. For me, it led to withdrawing from social contact, and I would try to hide my real feelings from those around me. It was a lot more than just a low mood – it seriously affected my physical and mental health – my behaviour, thoughts, and feelings, as well as my relationships. I know depression makes life difficult to manage from day to day for the sufferer, their family, and friends. It disconnects us from life. Depression is the leading cause of disability worldwide; sadly, it can often result in suicide. And from my perspective, it totally SUCKED!

The saddest thing for me is not really remembering a lot of my young girls' lives. We are now blessed to have three amazing young adults. We have just become step-grandparents and now have a gorgeous grandaughter, but the memories of my girls growing up are sadly a

bit foggy! As I share precious moments with our new grandchildren, I realise this is what my girls missed – or rather I missed. I was lucky to have evolved and grown somewhat by the time our son was born – our blessing doctors told me wouldn't be possible in my 30s because I had stressed my body so much that I had gone into menopause – once again I was able to totally reverse all this, much to our delight and the doctors' amazement.

You might think transforming depression into gold is impossible? You may ask, what is the point of even trying, why bother? I am sure I hear you saying, "To believe that I can feel happy is BS Tracey, you don't understand how I feel! The doctors have told me I will be fine if I just take antidepressants." Well this is BS, and are you really fine?? Ask yourself, if you really are fine and perfectly happy with where you are now, why are you reading this book? I want people to know that if I can do it, you too can become free from depression and heaviness, you can find yourself again, that inner spark, that lightness. And, in fact, you will find that the answers lie within you.

You CAN learn to believe in and connect with your true self, to transform your emotions and your despair into gold – to feel absolutely amazing! You can be the caterpillar turning within into a chrysalis and finally transforming into the beautiful butterfly!! Also think of how diamonds are formed – from deep pressure (de-press-ion)! You can be that diamond! IT ALL STARTS WITH YOU!

I have had many people tell me it is too hard or impossible, and sure, it is really hard; however, anything worth fighting for or achieving generally is. If you are reading this book,

then something has drawn you here. I feel you are open or willing to give things a go, and I write this book to empower you to say yes; follow your intuition that led you here! I hope to bring empowerment and inspiration to those currently **suffering** from "depression" (or any mental illness, affliction, or dis-ease at all really). Depression is indeed a very appropriate word as the word is depressing in itself, and you are causing yourself to suffer without knowing you have the ability to change things. It is not your fault that you didn't realise other possibilities existed; it is not your fault that you believed what you were told by mainstream opinion.

Depression is not some deep, dark monster to be ashamed of and pushed away. It is just your soul wanting you to acknowledge you are unbalanced, disconnected, and out of alignment. Your soul wants you to look at and heal these parts of yourself. Depression —what I like to call "it" – is an energy that can only be transformed by looking at "it", feeling "it", asking it questions, and recognising what "it" is trying to tell you. Have you heard the saying, questions are the answer? Well they truly are. If we can find the reasons or causes, we can collapse them, solve them, refine ourselves, and come to peace. Just like we can boil water, causing the water to transform into steam, we can do the same with depression – put it under some intense heat, and watch it transform into love and joy.

Depression is deep pressure you are putting on yourself, which, when released through transformation, allows you to ignite your inner spark, your gold, and enables you to find the brilliance of yourself and your life. To live a life worth fighting for and living so that you can be the best

you possible. To be loving and joyful. That is why you are here – to just be YOU.

I have now been "normal" (lol – whatever that is!) and happy, feeling fulfilled, for over 15 years. I have been off the meds for well over 20 years. Every day just gets better and better (of course there are ups and downs); however, I now have the tools and knowledge to ensure I can regain myself if I trip. I am able to continually improve myself, and I am bursting to show you what is possible.

I believe this book and my life experiences can help you too, especially if you feel, somewhere deep down inside, there is hope. If you are able to realise you have free will and can use this will to begin taking responsibility for yourself, to put in the required effort and work you will need to put in. If you are willing to go within and look at finding the causes, you will also receive the added benefit of building your natural immunity, aiding in preventing any further dis-ease and ill-health. These changes will allow you to be more open and will assist you to connect within to find your true and authentic self, so you can live an incredible life.

It is very important that you start slowly and gently when it comes to working on yourself; it is not a race, and it is better to cement changes in. When you think of all the pressure you have put on yourself over the years, we don't want to release that all at once and cause an explosion! So please let things flow rather than force them. And if you feel a bit overwhelmed, give yourself a rest, and just write about what is going on for you, or speak to someone who can be compassionate and understanding and help you through.

Even after dropping the meds, I still had years of hard knocks and realisations, ups and downs, to bring me to complete joy and gratitude for life (still, it was a lot less time than the time I had spent being miserable!) It was only my own resistance that delayed the process. I have to say I now have a hard time remembering and connecting with the feelings the old me had, as they are now gone. I am eternally grateful for my life, my learnings, and the fact I had and still have the rest of my life to enjoy!! Of course it has not been perfect all the way; however, it has been incredible, and I am excited for whatever is coming next. (As a sidebar, I don't recommend dropping your meds straight away like I did – this is recommended to be done slowly and with awareness.)

My Wish for You and Your Transformation

It is my wish to impart my knowledge to you and help make your journey swifter and easier in whatever way I can. I certainly took the hard road and know it can definitely be done a lot more quickly if you can make certain decisions and changes now, let go of resistance, and seek help and guidance. You don't have to do everything on your own. I also hope this book will bring all the different facets together for you so that you can see what is possible for you and begin your own journey to wellness. It will also give you some ideas to slowly begin with.

As I said previously, healing is very much about self-responsibility, so I recommend that you undertake whatever you can to the best of your ability. We are not aiming for a quick fix that temporarily solves the symptoms

without getting to the cause – we want to witness **what** was instrumental in causing the imbalance and transform it with love so that your mind, body, soul, and spirit can come back into balance. Your intention is everything.

There are so many things you can do to help yourself. Via this book, I want to give you a taste and get you thinking of how you can begin transforming now. This book is filled with practical, hands-on ways you can start with immediately. As a practising energy alchemist and therapist, I am able to assist you if you become stuck. If you resonate with my book and what I have to share, we will undoubtedly be a great fit to work together.

In reading this book, you might feel some things are confronting or confusing… this is all good… so please bear with me, and analyse those thoughts as they come – take your time to consider things, and reach out for help if you need it.

You may also feel as if you have read, seen, or heard all or some of this before, and you probably have as I have taken a lot of what I have learnt (which is tonnes!) and put it in here, so certainly a lot of my concepts are not original and have been known and practised for aeons.

One big difference is that it is easy to intellectually "know" something and quite another thing to be able to actually put that knowledge into practice!! I was the master at knowing and not doing!! However, I don't beat myself up about that like I used to, as I now know and believe that everything happens in perfect timing. I believe that by resonating with my message, it will bring you what you need to hear and enable you to take action.

I am definitely not perfect, I am human and want you to release any perfectionism you are holding onto to. I remember how much reading others' stories and what they discovered helped me to understand that I was not alone. Other people were going through the same feelings and experiences. Sometimes all it takes is one tiny nugget to really sink in and bring about huge transformation.

In reading this book you have choices – you can accept or reject what I have to say; however, please don't neglect it, and please at least give it some thought – for yourself!! Sometimes we don't know what we don't know – our unconscious mind is actually running the show.

Even now, I am constantly picking up books I read years ago, and it is like I have never seen them before – nothing rings a bell, and yet it is exactly what I needed to know at this moment. The fact is that unless you are ready for information, it will just go over your head, so be willing to change and release your resistance, as that will make things much easier. At least, you will be picking up the points you do need right now.

So, let's get on with it and **get you feeling better about yourself ASAP**. Mind you, that is a major key... feeling better about yourself because just as depression is all about you even when you get consumed with everyone else's life, so is your decision to get better all about you. You may even notice or admit to yourself that deep down you are wanting the attention or help of others despite your thinking the opposite is true. However your feelings are manifesting ultimately your decision to change starts with **YOU** and ends with **YOU**, it is all about **YOU**!

Your recovery depends totally on you coming to love and appreciate yourself. Not a self-centred, conceited love based on ego but a true love of who you are, the gifts you have, and the energy within you. (Listen to what your little voice is saying right now, I know mine used to want to be sick at the mention of the words self-love). Your self-worth – or rather lack of it, your little nagging voice, and your ego are the real drivers in this whole equation... Confronting... Yes, however, it is the truth. So let's lift the veil and begin the magic of your transformation...

You can consider that metamorphosis or transformation is truly possible, and what you might undergo is like the process of a butterfly becoming, coming to be. A caterpillar starts as an egg (you are the egg), breaks out of that shell (you decide to change and break out from where you are now), eats his shell, and then proceeds to eat leaves, a lot of leaves, to give him energy for the journey ahead. Like the caterpillar, you become bigger and stronger and are able to shed your old form – as you enter your chrysalis, you actually digest and rebuild yourself so that you can emerge as a beautiful butterfly. It takes a lot of work and self-reflection to discover how, what, why, and when you became depressed – you literally eat yourself and consume new information. This will be your transformation! Remember also that in the end, though others can certainly help you, no one else can bring you out of that chrysalis – it is up to you!

Something also worth considering is that your transformation can have rippling effects throughout the world, for we are all one. Heal yourself, and you will help heal oth-

ers as well. This has definitely helped me during the hard times.

> *"Personal transformation can and does have global effects. As we go, so goes the world, for the world is us. The revolution that will save the world is ultimately a personal one."*
>
> —*Marianne Williamson*

So if you have ever wanted to save others, you may now realise it all begins with saving yourself first! Let's get into it!

Chapter 1

Acceptance and Commitment

"I see myself living a life where I am not bound by the opinions others have of me, one where I no longer concern myself with the judgements of others, one in which I believe in myself and my talents, skills and capabilities. I imagine, and therefore bring about, a life where I do not need to justify my existence, where I am free to be who I really am."

—Michael Rawls

We are all Different – Accept Yourself and Where You are at

You are perfect as you are – each of us is different in our own way – like little pieces of coral – all distinct. Like no thumbprint is ever the same, never are we the same as another human being. What a lot of us do have in common though, is that we like to fool ourselves into thinking we are less than the perfection we are. We let others influence us with their thoughts and beliefs, and we often belittle ourselves with our own thinking. We are often stuck in FOG (Fear, Obligation, and Guilt), which drives so many of us to forget who we are (perfect) and why we are here

(to have fun, feel joy, and love ourselves and others). We cannot make mistakes if we learn to follow our own inner guidance and what brings us (not others) happiness.

It feels like I have been on a rollercoaster my whole life, always doubting myself so much so that decisions were difficult. I spent most of my life trying to be someone else and trying to please others – in the meantime, mostly hating and despising myself for the failure I saw myself as. My self-hate even meant I hated having my photo taken or looking at photos of myself – I always thought they were terrible. I have learnt it is virtually impossible to live up to everyone else's expectations without little regard for your own. I have been where I put myself – unhappy, ungrateful, depressed, a drama queen, a financial failure.

Since coming to realise the profoundness of what I am about to tell you, my life has totally turned around, and yours can too, if you learn to accept, love, and forgive yourself and become truly grateful for your life. I am not talking about a vain love but a love born of appreciation and gratitude for the gifts you have been given, for the uniqueness of you. It is a different kind of love, not boastful or unkind, and it guides you to constantly make the right choices for you without feeling guilt, embarrassment, or shame.

Accept and acknowledge yourself for who and what you are – where you are at in this moment – and commit to following what feels right for you. Then you will feel unsurpassed happiness, gratitude, and confidence in who you are. You will embody a calming inner peace that brings vitality, life force. You will no longer try to escape pain as

you now know that you matter. You will be separate from old pain and connected within yourself.

Do not accept what is and say things to yourself like, "That's just life" or "Life isn't fair", as life is fair – it is just trying to reveal something to you. Do not accept that you cannot heal if someone tells you this. Accept that it is possible to transform and release past and present hurts and trauma. **YOU CAN HEAL!**

Mainstream doctors, media, and general societal thinking teach us that change is not possible. However, we are always changing; we are not a solid physical presence as we might think. We are energy, constantly changing and moving, and we cannot stay as we are (as some may tend to believe). You can choose to go one way or the other, that is the only choice. As change is inevitable, you can grow or decay, so make growth your choice!

Have a Clear Intention, Decide to Heal, and Follow Your Intuition

It makes things a lot easier if you have a clear intention of what you want to achieve to start with. I am going to give you a lot of information; however, I want you to do what feels "right" for you – this is hugely different from doing things because you feel obligated or that you "should". When you do something from guilt, obligation, or fear, it feels wrong, and it is hard to move forward.

There is a difference between stretching yourself and it ultimately feeling good for you (even if it does bring up emotion) and stretching yourself and it feeling bad and

out of whack. Just doing what you are told usually results in disaster – that I can definitely vouch for. If it is wrong for you, you will feel the uncomfortable force, and the depression will worsen, as it did for me on meds. I have been to plenty of doctors, studied many self-help techniques, and learnt from masters, financial mentors, and coaches. And I can now notice that I feel a huge difference when something is not in my best interest, no matter what they might suggest or tell me. Use your discretion, be discerning, and follow your inner wisdom and intuition.

People need to do things for themselves. You will need to step up and own your stuff. No one else can take on this journey for you. You can ask for help, guidance, and advice (which I encourage you to do), but ultimately it is you who has to do the work. **You need to commit to yourself**. It is going to take patience, courage, discipline, and compassion for yourself. You need to trust that you are worthy and deserving of this. If you want to pretend to yourself that you are doing the work while you are not really getting involved or feeling it as deeply as you could be, or you're skipping steps, then it is just going to take you a lot longer. Resistance is your refusal to acknowledge what is really going on.

For example, I never could visualise, but I used to pretend I could so that I didn't look silly. I wanted to fit in rather than be honest and ask if there was another way I could sense things. I spent so much time worrying about the fact that I couldn't visualise. When I was finally able to realise there was nothing wrong with me, I found I have inner knowing and feeling instead of actual vision, and this is great. This enabled me to focus on what I could perceive rather than

worrying about what I couldn't. Some people hear things, they have auditory awareness. Find what works for you, and don't be embarrassed if something doesn't work for you – there is always another way.

We are all different and don't have to be the same. I would affirm myself till I was blue in the face, never believing a lot of it, as I hadn't realised or released my limited beliefs. I was afraid to ask for help for fear of looking silly. So if you feel blocked, ask for some guidance, and then feel if the suggestions are right for you.

Financially we gave everything away because neither my husband nor myself believed in ourselves enough to make our own decisions or follow our intuition – we thought it better to seek an expert who could tell us what to do. I underwent many years of depression – what for?? All I was doing was constantly beating myself up, thinking I was never good enough and couldn't do what was required of me. I was worried about how people saw me and the fact that I felt they never heard or listened to me.

I found that my depression was an obsession with myself. I felt such despair through my obsession with comparing myself to others and seeing them as perfect, unlike me. If they displayed traits that I disliked, I would judge them. I didn't realise this was how I judged myself; the traits I disliked in them were what I disliked in myself. I was stuck in these feelings. And by trying to escape my feelings and thoughts about these unwanted traits, I continually made them worse rather than accepting and transforming them by seeing and acknowledging them in myself. My ego was running the show. Sometimes I would be able to escape

my thoughts and feelings; however, without transforming them, they inevitably returned with even more force.

One of the best decisions I ever made in my life was that I was not going to be this label of "severely depressed" that I had been given and that I would find another way to help myself heal and become free. Instead of feeling trapped, I wanted to transform the depression into freedom, love, and joy. I remember as a young teenager looking out the window and wanting to be free – can you remember what you wanted from life?

After having acknowledged and accepted where you are at, the first step to transformation is to make a decision from the current FOG you are in. A decision to change. I know depression may seem like it is not a choice, but you can decide to get better and heal yourself. You may not even believe it is possible for you to heal – all I am asking is for you to consider it possible, take the first step, and give it a go. This will take some self-confidence and resilience as you need to push through the current dark cloud. Believe me, I know the hardest thing to do is to take affirmative action when you feel like crap, but it is worth it. *YOU ARE WORTH IT!*

Get Out of Your Head, Ground Yourself and Become Present

Another tip is that "problems can't be solved with the same thinking that caused them". You need to somehow find a way to get out of your head (which is just a tool to be used to help us in our lives – not to run our lives) and get into your heart. You need to become curious about

yourself and your behaviour rather than push yourself away. Hopefully by the end of this book, you will be able to get out of your mind and into your heart, or, even better, learn to connect your heart, mind, body, and soul so that you can become one within, no longer a scattered version of you.

Can you accept where you are and who you are at this point in time? Accept, not settle! Do you have any idea where you would like to be, how you would like to feel? Focus on this. You need to commit to yourself and get a bit clear so that you can focus on changing what is weighing you down. De-press-ion is a weight. It is deep pressure you are placing on yourself to be someone you are not. That is why you feel miserable. Because your soul is trying to tell you this is not who you are. However, like a diamond, it is this pressure that will mould you into your brilliance. It is time to stop resisting yourself. Time to let go of the old thoughts, patterns, beliefs, and ways of being. To transform the fear of others seeing the real us into feeling proud of who we are and hoping they do see us and we see ourselves.

The cause of so much of our pain and suffering is a result of our wandering mind focusing on things that aren't present. We need to become aware of our mind and become present – that is the gift! If you are feeling your body, paying attention to your body, and feeling your energy within, then your mind is present. A great tool is to ground yourself. Let your feet feel heavy, and imagine roots growing out of your feet, sinking into the Earth, deepening like those of an old fig tree, enabling you to become grounded and unshakeable. When you are grounded like this, take slow deep breaths into

your abdomen, and when you exhale, send your intention and awareness into the Earth. When you inhale, you bring in inspiration and creativity. You become aware of yourself; you can observe your mind, language, and behaviour, and from there you can take a different path than the one you were previously on.

The Answer Lies Within You and Your Conscious/Unconscious Mind

The secret is to know that the answer lies within YOU – it has always been there. We need to find you. You need to realise who you are and just BE YOU. We need to connect with ourselves to change our old conditioning and ways of being. Take back your power and become your authentic, true self. It all starts with you!!

The biggest hurdle I have found with myself and my clients is accepting this – the truth that you are so powerful – you are the most powerful force in your life – you can create anything! It is also the reason so many of us drink, smoke, or indulge in other habits or addictions. To escape and avoid this connection. We become afraid of our power, but we don't need to be. We allow our mind to take control and wander into the past, which just recreates our past into our future, and nothing changes. The story may change, but the basic tenet is the same, "I am a failure, not good enough, no one loves me..." We need to put an end to this and create a new, exciting, and compelling future.

You will always find what you are looking for or seeing in yourself. If you think you aren't worthy, you will attract people to confirm that for you. If you think no one apart

from you is capable of doing something, you won't find capable people who can help you.

You will never change your life until you decide you are worth the time and effort and until you start to change some of your daily habits, routines, thoughts, feelings, words, and actions. When we do this, we can get out of our own way and be in flow and connection. There will be times when this is hard, and you won't feel like continuing, and people might tell you it's a bad time to be doing this. This is when you need to realise you are worth it, and you can do this! The Universe and I have your back. Once you make the decision and stand firm, the path clears. We really do have everything we need within to grow on a personal level. Every thought and feeling you have will have a direct impact on your body – on your health and wellbeing.

Your unconscious mind is often really running the show. You might make a conscious decision to change and do things differently, but the outcome may be totally different than what you initially envisaged. This can sometimes happen due to fear; for example, your goal might be to stop drinking every night, but if your unconscious mind fears that you will have to face certain emotions or miss out on something, it can override your conscious decision and cause you to fail to keep you 'safe'. This is a form of avoidance – it is easier to stay on the path you are on, keep hidden, and avoid the issues rather than confront what is really running the show.

It can also be due to what we call "secondary gains" – the gains you will receive from having that drink, such as when relaxation and the ability to switch off outweigh the gain

of wanting to change that habit and be healthier. Some of these secondary gains can be hard to admit and face. You have to take a good hard look at yourself to uncover them. Another secondary gain may be that you can avoid responsibility – "I can't do whatever…. I have depression." It may sometimes be easier to take a pill than confront issues, and the medication brings the gain of feeling better pretty well immediately. Although I have to say that when you face and transform your issues, these changes are far more longstanding and enjoyable.

Maybe you get extra attention or love from family and friends by being depressed or ill. Maybe it is just safer to stay in or hide in your comfort zone. At times the gain may be that you want to make someone else feel guilty – "You did this to me by betraying, leaving, abandoning, or hurting me". Sometimes (sadly), we just want to opt out of life, and this is easier than facing ourselves and explaining to people what is really going on. You may feel you are your depression, and it gives you an excuse and a way of punishing yourself. You may enjoy the drama or see some other sort of benefit. There are so many reasons we don't escape our pain because it brings us some sort of secondary gain, pleasure, or avoidance on some level.

Your conscious mind is aware of everything around you at every moment. It is logical and practical. However, it is like the tip of an iceberg, and the unconscious (subconscious) mind is the submerged part of the iceberg – the largest part – it is more intuitive and emotional. Say you have had a breakup, and your conscious mind is now saying, "I do not want to be alone". However, the subconscious cannot process negatives and only hears, "I want to be alone", so

it will bring you experiences to ensure you remain "alone". It will bring you whatever you are focusing on. If you are focusing on debt, it will bring you more debt to please you. If you are focusing on unhappiness, it will bring you more of that too. You are a spider's web in action, catching whatever you are thinking about. If you believe you can't transform yourself, you will catch things to show you you can't, such as other people saying it isn't possible.

So it is extremely important to direct your subconscious mind with focus on what you DO WANT – have a clear intention and confidence that you will succeed. Do this with purpose and direction so that when you look at your life in a year's time, you will be astounded at how far you have come. Let go of any fear of failure. I would far more fear staying in the same place you are in now, which we now know is not possible – that means you will be going backwards into decay – eek! My goal is for you to really want to transform your depression (which is actually a type of addiction) and the habits that keep you in this state of being into the energy of love and joy, so you can find YOUR inner spark.

You will need to accept, be committed, and embrace the fact that... transformation isn't going to be all beer and skittles. You may at times have to face some dark and murky places to give birth to yourself. You are going to have to find, feel and acknowledge the untruths you have been carrying in your body and face those demons. It will only be difficult if you resist the process. Hold the butterfly in your thoughts.

Let's Begin the Transformation Process

To begin transforming we are going to need clarity and focus, which will entail the following:

- Take this slowly, one step at a time. This is not a book to be rushed, so please go slowly, deliberately, and with contemplation. Be happy with the small achievements, and cement those in as you strengthen your sense of self – what we call our "I AM" – "I AM enough, I AM powerful, I AM loved". Notice how you feel saying that. If you can't feel it at this stage, just go with it and give it a whirl for now.

- Please stay on any medications at first, but be aware that they often dumb you down and keep you numb, so as you feel better, seek assistance in easing off them.

- A journal for writing in as much as you are able – I found each day a bit much for a long time; however, once I realised how much it helped, it made it a lot easier to commit to the process. Find a journal that resonates with you, that is beautiful and makes you feel powerful. It is great to go back to these later to see how far you have really come. I have only just started keeping mine and regret not doing so sooner.

- Commitment – realise you want to change, you have decided to change. And choose to commit and succeed.

- Belief, faith, desire, intent, and willingness that you can do this – even if it is wobbly to start with – just know you got this! It is ok to make mistakes.

- You are going to need to be a stand for yourself and place boundaries around yourself. You will need some space and some support. If you slip, that is fine – get up again as soon as you can. My mistake was often wallowing in my emotions, letting them overtake me again, and not reaching out for help.

- To release and transform resistance in the form of "I can't" or "It's too hard" into "I got this"!!!!! If you find you are resisting the present moment, then stop what you are doing, and breathe slowly and deeply into your belly, which will elevate your energy and relax and calm your mind.

- This is probably the most important! To realise there is NOTHING wrong with you. You are just in a bad place at the moment and can move by a little wiggle at a time. You are going to be so damn proud of yourself when you are done!

The Benefits of Transformation

Through the process of choosing transformation and love for yourself, you are going to truly discover gold in yourself, your relationship with yourself, and your place in the world. Some things you will learn are to:

- Accept yourself – all of yourself – including the dark parts you never wanted to acknowledge – so that acceptance becomes appreciation and celebration

- Know what you truly want
- Change the way you think, feel, and act, what you say, and how you say it
- Release feelings of overwhelm
- Change your posture and the way you breathe and hold yourself
- Turn your focus from self-hate and self-criticism to self-love
- Increase your confidence
- Have deeper and more fulfilling relationships
- Realise that emotions are e-motion – energy in motion, and it is ok to feel them but not be consumed by them
- Increase energy and motivation
- Transform old feelings of lack and powerlessness
- Embrace and be grateful for your previous suffering – heal your pain
- Live in the present
- Let go of worry and FOG (fear, obligation, and guilt), and while we are at it, shame, blame, etc. – I could go on forever!
- Allow yourself to be happy and to really LAUGH and feel awesome about it
- Allow others to see who you truly are and feel safe in doing so
- Build your confidence that change is possible with small steps
- Safely and lovingly face your demons by connecting to yourself and your soul, spirit, or Higher Self
- Gain clarity and focus for yourself and your life
- Find forgiveness for yourself and others
- Connect within and with others

- Uproot and replace old beliefs and judgements holding you back
- Receive more financial abundance via the way you are now vibrating and attracting
- Regain your health
- Remember who you really are, and take your place as a shining light in the world
- Regain trust in yourself and others
- Feel fulfilled
- Make peace with the past and even be grateful for the things you used to hate
- Inspire others to do what you have done
- Be inspired yourself
- Raise consciousness throughout the planet, as we are all connected
- Be truly amazed at what you are capable of!!

These are just a few of the benefits, plus who knows what else you may be able to learn and achieve!

"All our dreams can come true, if we have the courage to pursue them."

—Walt Disney

Follow-Up Exercises – Intentions

- Commit to your journey, your healing, and transforming your life. Go out and buy yourself a journal now – one that you love the look and feel of, and start contemplating what you would like for your life. If you are living out in the country, like I initially was, start writing in whatever you have available now and order something beautiful online. (I intend to also produce a journal in the near future.)

- Grab a cuppa, go somewhere you can be undisturbed, preferably out in nature, but if that's not possible, find a place in the house where you feel comfortable. Ground yourself as I described earlier. Relax and connect within as much as possible, and write your intentions for your life – see if you can start to feel excited about what might be possible?

- Can you recognise and acknowledge (without judging yourself) anything you may have been avoiding or any secondary gains you may be receiving by remaining as you are?

- Start telling a better-feeling story about the things that are important to you. What could be possible for your life? Tell an uplifting, magical story of what could happen. Let go of any voices that might start weighing up the pros and cons or bringing up what did or didn't happen in the past. Let yourself dream!

"Things never happen by accident. They happen because you have a vision, you have a commitment and you have a dream"

—*Osca de la Renta*

My intention for you via this book is that you will learn how to connect with your higher self and have a massive breakthrough in your life. It means being open, trusting, surrendering and allowing your true self to shine through.

Take Back Your Power With Energy Consciousness

"You have power over your mind - not outside events. Realise this, and you will find strength."
—*Marcus Aurelius*

You are Powerful! I cannot emphasise that enough! You might think you are powerless – you are most definitely not. You are the one with all the power, you have just hidden it from yourself. Can you analyse your point of view, your perspective of yourself? What are you saying about yourself, to yourself? I bet you wouldn't talk to anyone else that way, and if you did, imagine how they would feel!

Can you tell that nagging, incessant, little voice to be quiet for a moment? Can you even allow yourself to dream you can be happy? Can you fathom that most of the voices in your head are just that, voices, and they probably aren't telling you the truth? Can you thank them, let them pass by like clouds floating overhead and then tell yourself a different story?

There is No Separation – Except in our Mind – Energy Follows Thoughts

It is important to remember that even though at times it might not seem like it, we are never separated from our inner self, our God within, as there is only oneness, light, love. We need to remove our thinking brain and come from our heart. When you live in and from your heart, you will feel with more love. You will know and believe that you are safe and protected. You will trust in the Universe and accept yourself. There is no good or bad, there just is. It is our mind that tricks us. The only separation in ourselves is in our mind.

Energy follows thought. So watch your thoughts!

In Dr David Hawkins' book "Power vs Force: The Hidden Determinants of Human Behaviour", he discusses how power and force, respectively, affect our thoughts, emotions, and actions. He talks about how we can increase our level of power and reduce our reliance on force (I see the force as my constant attempts to control myself and others which saw me only going further down the scale). Every act, thought, and choice – our decisions – can affect not only our life but the lives of everyone. We think we live by forces we control, but in fact we are governed by power from unrevealed sources.

Map of Consciousness

Depression is an energy. We are all made of energy and vibration. Have you seen the map of consciousness developed by Dr Hawkins? There are many maps and scales available, so if this one doesn't resonate with you search the internet to find one that does. Or even better, make up your own scale of where you are now emotionally or physically and where you would like to go. Please take some time to study this, and let it sink into your subconscious. Once you embrace this scale, you are aware. And if you slip back, which does happen, you can work on moving back up again.

I have also put a reference to this in the appendix, as we will be referring to it often.

Map of Consciousness

Developed By David R. Hawkins

	Name of Level	Energetic Log	Predominant Emotional State	View of Life	God-view	Process
Spiritual Paradigm	Enlightenment	700-1000	Ineffable	Is	Self	Pure Consciousness
	Peace	600	Bliss	Perfect	All-Being	Illumination
	Joy	540	Serenity	Complete	One	Transfiguration
	Love	500	Reverence	Benign	Loving	Revelation
Reason & Integrity	Reason	400	Understanding	Meaningful	Wise	Abstraction
	Acceptance	350	Forgiveness	Harmonious	Merciful	Transcendence
	Willingness	310	Optimism	Hopeful	Inspiring	Intention
	Neutrality	250	Trust	Satisfactory	Enabling	Release
	Courage	200	Affirmation	Feasible	Permitting	Empowerment
Survival Paradigm	Pride	175	Scorn	Demanding	Indifferent	Inflation
	Anger	150	Hate	Antagonistic	Vengeful	Aggression
	Desire	125	Craving	Disappointing	Denying	Enslavement
	Fear	100	Anxiety	Frightening	Punitive	Withdrawal
	Grief	75	Regret	Tragic	Disdainful	Despondency
	Apathy	50	Despair	Hopeless	Condemning	Abdication
	Guilt	30	Blame	Evil	Vindictive	Destruction
	Shame	20	Humiliation	Miserable	Despising	Elimination

I imagine if you are reading this book, you are currently living in the survival paradigm as I was, I was down the bottom level of shame. You are going to raise your vibration from wherever you currently sit on the scale up to love, from survival to spiritual. It is all about learning to accept and love yourself – without settling for any less. It is all about choosing love, peace, and joy for your life – well and even perhaps enlightenment! I do kind of feel, though, that once you get to this stage, you might well go "poof" into the ether!

My wish for you is that YOU will find and love the REAL you – not the you that is the mask you present to others. You want to raise your energy and transform those old hopeless feelings into love and joy. Remember who you are – you are energy – light – life force. Via depression we have wallowed in our darkness and turned out our light. We need to reclaim this light and balance the light with the dark to find ourselves. We don't get rid of the darkness, we accept it and transform it from powerless into powerful, from victim into victorious.

To climb this scale, we need to examine our subconscious mind. This means you will need to go back to basics and make the changes that you can, when and where you can. If you happen to slip back down the ladder, do not judge yourself; just climb back on and continue holding your intentions firm or find someone who can take your hand and help you back up. Take it step by step. Remember to be gentle on yourself and that this is not a race.

Your subconscious contains repressed memories, so we need to release the unwanted feelings at the lower end

of the emotional scale by recalling and examining these memories in a way that is safe for you and will allow you to rid yourself of all trapped emotions. Like a snake shedding its skin, there is a letting go process required to become the best version of yourself. This is extremely freeing! We often bury our emotions and memories as we are afraid to deal with them, and they then lead to ill-health, dis-ease (not being at ease with yourself), physical injuries and maladies, anxiety, and depression (deep pressure).

As you climb the scale and step up the ladder a strength of will grows within you and you are better able to deal with crisis. You realise there is something within you that means the external cannot crush your inner foundations. You will find your inner strength, courage and potential as you face any external issues from a higher place of inner confidence and knowing.

Observation Without Judgement

By observing our memories, allowing them to float to the surface, we can deal with the associated emotions, even the most painful ones. We can become responsible for ourselves rather than blaming others or, worse still, blaming and bullying ourselves. If we are caught in our own problems and self-judgement, we can project these onto others, and our beliefs about ourselves and the world can become rampantly vicious. We can assume and draw hasty and wrong conclusions. We can believe these assumptions are true, but that is, more often than not, not the case. We can become defensive and withdrawn rather than see the real truth and find a solution. It is important to be able to look at what we have done or experienced in

the past and respect and appreciate that so we can move forward.

We need to occupy your mind to keep it out of mischief and give it things to do to redirect it to more positive and productive goals. Your mind is a tool that you need to learn how to use. That is why it is so important to identify and accept exactly where you are, what you want, and where you want to go. You can then instruct your mind and connect with the real you to take yourself on the ride of your life. Imagine being at the end of your life and being proud to tell others what you have achieved and how you made the most of your life. Imagine being able to share your story and inspire others. Maybe even to leave a legacy!

Expansion, Vibration and Energy

"If we do not believe within ourselves this deeply rooted feeling that there is something higher than ourselves, we shall never find the strength to evolve into something higher."

—Rudolf Steiner

When you start to change your frequency and vibration, you will change your life. You are now constantly moving up the map of consciousness and changing your energy (your life force, your Qi/Chi) and what you attract in life. As mentioned earlier, depression is an energy, and we are changing that energy. Often when it comes to depression, people mostly discuss issues that relate to your physical and mental states or what is going on chemically within your body. Now, I believe an unseen aspect that has a

huge influence and that many people are unaware of is the spiritual side of things, the energy side. This is the part I have really come to love – resetting our energy and getting into a flow state. Being able to let go and get out of our head, into our heart, and out of our own way.

This is where your inner child gets to play, to sing, dance, and be creative. I love listening to the joy of the kookaburras singing, and I remember to laugh and feel joy each day. This is where you come back to the essence of who you really are and allow yourself to flourish. This is where you make your mark in the world and find true love and happiness.

We need to learn to trust ourselves, realise there is only abundance, find our power, and expand our energy and vibration that we send out to the world. If you're breathing, you have power. We are power – we are energy, we are vibration. Step into your expansion, and expand your awareness. What is the message you are giving out to the world – what are you vibrating now? Be discerning about where your energy is going! Have you noticed any change in your energy since realising that transformation is possible?

One of my favourite books that really proved to me that anything is possible and there really is a spiritual side to life is "Dying to Be Me" by Anita Moorjani. This inspirational memoir describes how after fighting cancer for almost four years – doing what everyone else wanted her to do – her body began shutting down, and she had a near-death experience where she finally realised her inner worth. She

awakened to the fact that not being aware of or listening to her Higher Self was the reason for her dis-ease.

I truly believe illness, like depression, is generally a "dis-ease" (an uneasiness) within ourselves. Anita affirmed for me that we are all spiritual beings having a human experience, and the only person you need to be is yourself. What she shared with the world spoke to me from a perspective of depression as I too was doing what everyone else wanted me to do, not realising or appreciating my inner worth, not looking after my energy body, and not connecting with my spiritual side. It really helped me to see that the only person I need to be or listen to is myself.

I feel that accidents, illnesses, loss of security and death are the things that lead us down our spiritual path if that is wanted by our soul. They help us to awaken, to ask the big questions and look at life in a different way. When we ignore these signals we lose sight of the bigger picture and what we are being shown.

Understanding Our Energy Bodies' Connection to Depression

On a very basic level we are made up of energy lines called meridians which correspond to our main organs, spinning vortexes of energy points called chakras, and an aura made of seven different energy bodies surrounding our physical body. These energy bodies are also connected to our main seven chakras. Our chakras bring our vital energy. Our aura's subtle bodies can be seen by some individuals or by using Kirlian Camera Imaging. When you go for acupuncture, the needles are placed along

the meridian line points. In kinesiology, we also use these points, rubbing or holding them to shift energy.

I will just touch briefly on this subject as whole books can be written about our meridians, aura, and chakras. Chakras are energy centres running through our body. They are characterised by seven colours. We carry many things in our chakras, including our sense of security, our desires, our sense of purpose, our ability to speak up, and our self-worth. As an energy healer, I often feel or sense symbols, colours, shadows, objects, denseness, archetypes, emotions, images, words, or people within a person's chakras, revealing what may be within their energy field.

You may have heard the expression or seen the ancient Chinese symbol yin-yang, representing opposing forces that are also interconnected and counterbalancing. These forces are within us; light and dark, day and night, good and evil, as above, so below, as within, so without, and our masculine and feminine energies. So when depressed, we may often find our male and female sides, our yin-yang, are unbalanced. We need to accept and embrace all parts of ourself in order to be balanced. We can often find these aspects of ourselves within our chakras, or they may show as an imbalance on one side of the body.

Our aura is like a protective energetic shield around us. It is affected by our mood and emotional state, and sometimes the states of others. Different colours of the aura are associated with different qualities and emotions. These layers reflect what is happening in your material, physical world. This can include your inner health – how

you think and feel about yourself, your life, and the world. It can also reflect how you experience pain. Your ability to heal and overcome the physical is shown through your aura. Higher layers are connected to your soul and your ego, your focus on the sensual pleasures of life, especially with regards to sex, food, drink, and alcohol, rather than the spiritual. It can also reflect your childhood experiences and your ability to grow and acquire loving wisdom.

All plants, animals, and humans have an aura – even inanimate objects still vibrate. In a healthy state, the entire aura can extend several feet out from your physical body and is very bright in colour. In an unhealthy or weakened state, the auric field can be quite small and dull, even damaged. When you pick up someone's vibe, you are generally tuning into their aura. You can also feel your own energy field by simply rubbing your hands together for about 10 seconds and then slowly separating them from each other. That buzzing is your energy. Animals are especially great at picking up on that energy and behaving accordingly. You will find if you are tired and run down, ungrounded, or not protecting your energy field, you can also pick up other people's frazzled or angry, sad energy, and if you are feeling upbeat at the time, they can also drain your energy, leaving you depleted.

Our meridian energy lines, chakra points, and auras can become blocked and damaged; however, we are able to work on them and clear them with various techniques, including sounds, colour, light, symbols, sacred geometry, and love, which all vibrate at a high-level frequency. The effects of blockages or stagnant energy, or sometimes

entities, within our chakras, meridians, and aura can play an immense role in our body and our state of being.

Some people find it hard to believe that our energy can affect us so strongly; however, I liken it to mental illness – you cannot see it, yet you can truly feel the effects of it! When we tune into this energy and clear the blockages or entities, the changes in our mental health can be massive. Just as Einstein discovered, we are all energy in motion. We are all made up of a mass of vibrating atoms moving at the speed of light and emitting frequencies, ie. $E=MC^2$. To ultimately heal, we need to raise those vibrations and frequencies and bring more love in.

Self-Protection Methods

As I mentioned, it is very important to protect our energy so that we don't take on the energy of others. There are many ways we can do this.

I like to ground myself (imagine my feet are roots going into the Earth) and then "zip myself up" or imagine I am in a five-pointed star or being washed over by a shower of brilliant light.

Cold water is amazing for clearing, a cold shower or a dip in the ocean can do wonders for your aura and hence your energy field.

We can also clear and transmute stagnant energy through gentle movement, intention, or other means, as mentioned above. We can always connect with the Universe above ourselves and bring in clean and clearing energy, and we can send the old heavy energy to the Earth

below or imagine it transforming into beautiful butterflies. The best thing is this is absolutely free and can be done in an instant. Taking old energy and sending it back to the Earth to compost and grow it into something new is also a lovely image, as is sending it into an imaginary fire.

Use the technique that resonates with you. Just ensure you put the fire out, and never send old energy to someone else. Our intention is always to transmute or transform it with absolute love and light.

Other things that can affect your energy are energy parasites, which can be in the form of people, places, or events. I think at this time, the mainstream media are also a type of energy parasite, bringing constant doom and gloom and sending people into fear. Medications and other medical interventions can negatively affect your energy field. Energy parasites can also be in the form of beliefs, words, or thoughts you may have or may have received. They can sit in your organs, chakras, aura, or other places within your body. With Energy Reset (another wonderful modality I have learnt), we can release these parasites, reset your aura and energy field, and restart your life in a new and higher frequency with a new intention.

During this time of world upheaval and attempted government control, many people have been affected by the energy within the world. Some have awakened to realise that they can make a difference in this world, as indeed I feel I have awakened and been drawn to help myself and others. Thus it is especially important for us all to become self-responsible and heal ourselves. Unfortunately others have gone into fear and indifference, and that is their

choice. If you are reading this, I hope it will inspire you to discover that you too can raise the consciousness of the planet and humanity by becoming all you can be. I feel we are returning to ancient and proven ways of healing.

Follow-Up Exercises – Where You Are at Now and Where You Want to Go

To accept where you currently are and where you want to go, I found the following really helpful to journal with – please go slowly, and be kind with yourself.

Relax and let it flow – try not to take it too seriously. Make sure you keep a copy that you can refer to later. It is great to see how far you have come.

Please just make a decision that you ARE worthy and deserving of taking the time to go through these exercises. When I started I wasn't really sure what I wanted, as I didn't know who I was at all. So this can be an ever-evolving process. Just do your best:

- Note where you currently are at as per the Map of Consciousness above. Journal about how you currently feel and what is going on for you and in your life.

- Answer these questions, where 10 is excited, and 1 is not at all excited. On a scale of 1 to 10...
  What is your level of interest in doing things?
  How do you feel about yourself?
  What is your level of energy?
  How much energy do you have in the day?

What is your sleep like?
How much do you exercise?
How deep and calm is your breathing?
What is your posture like?
What is your memory like?
How is your appetite level?
How are your concentration levels?
Are you fidgety or restless, or just plain exhausted?
Do you feel excited about life?
How much time do you spend scrolling through social media?

•   Take a photo of yourself as you are now, and record your weight.

•   Write a statement of how you want to feel and look, who you want to be, what you want to do, what you would like to have – what you want from life. If it is hazy and you are unsure, just make a start and work on getting into the feeling of those things. If you just can't be bothered doing this at this point in time, then ask yourself when was the very first time you felt apathetic like this – what was going on? Just start writing, and see what comes out.

•   Ask yourself, are there any reasons you might not want to change? And what might it feel like if you stay as you are now? Journal about this. For example, by staying unhappy and on meds, you might get to avoid being responsible for yourself or others.

•   If you don't change now, how will your life look in 1-5 or 10 years' time?

- If you are able to transform, how might that look and feel over the same time span?

- Concentrate on wanting to feel better, and ask for help from whoever or whatever you believe in. Even start with "Please help me to feel better" or "How can I feel better?" You might be surprised at what suddenly crosses your path! So stay on the lookout for who or what might show up.

- When you get some answers around this, you can then ask, "What is this depression trying to tell me?" Even though you might not know who you are actually speaking to, your inner self will guide you to what you need. It is great to do this before you go to sleep, as well as in the morning and through the day.

- What is the message you are giving out to the world – what are you vibrating now? Have you noticed any change in your energy since realising that transformation is possible?

- Practise the self-protection exercises – find one that resonates with you.

- What energy parasites might be in your field or drawing on your power? How might you address these issues?

- What new, empowering, and uplifting intentions can you bring into your life?

Just remember...

"It does not matter how slowly you go as long as you do not stop."

—*Confucius*

And I might add… as long as you make a start – you will be so proud of yourself for that small step into finding yourself!

Chapter 3

Nourishment and Tools for Your Body, Mind, Spirit and Soul

"Happiness is impermanent, like everything else. In order for happiness to be extended and renewed, you have to learn how to feed your happiness. Nothing can survive without food, including happiness; your happiness can die if you don't know how to nourish it. If you cut a flower but you don't put it in some water, the flower will wilt in a few hours. Even if happiness is already manifesting, we have to continue to nourish it."

—*Thich Nhat Hanh*

If I have learnt anything, it is how important it is to commit to nourishing your body, mind, spirit, and soul in as many ways as possible. When we are in the hole of depression, we really aren't caring for ourself at all, which is part of the reason we feel so bad. The main reason for this is our total lack of self-esteem. As I have said, we are all different, so your experiences are undoubtedly going to differ from mine; however, some of the things I am sharing, I have found to be quite common amongst depressed clients, and it might just open your mind to things that might be affecting you.

Back to Basics – Food, Nutrition and Household Products

I am going to start with the basics, with where I started, which gave me my immediate health back, and gave me energy and belief. The first thing that came into my world when I asked within for help was from a friend who rang me out of the blue, offering supplements, nutritionals, and chemical-free household products.

At first I loathed taking her up on the offer. I didn't really want to see anyone for a start, let alone get involved in network marketing, which is what the company was. However, something kept niggling at me (which I later learnt was my intuition and my energetic helpers answering my call for help). Living on the land (at the time we lived on a station in North West Queensland), I knew how depleted our soils are and the fact that our food is not bringing us the nutrition we need. Our soils, food, and animals are also being poisoned with chemicals, medicines, and vaccinations – just as we are.

So I faced my demons and asked her around to show me everything she had to offer. I bought the whole lot, and it totally changed how I felt. I threw out all my household goodies laden with chemicals and replaced them with chemical-free products. The whole family also started on the nutritional products – vitamins, minerals, antioxidants, probiotics, and essential fatty acids. Not only did I feel a lot better – we all did.

What Else Could Be Affecting Your Health and Wellbeing?

Many years later, when I went back into a bit of a slump (after not nourishing myself as I had been), I discovered via a holistic doctor that I (and the kids) have a condition called pyrrole disorder. This basically means our body doesn't store zinc and B6, and we need to replenish these on a daily basis. According to fxmedicine.com. au, "Pyrrole disorder affects up to 10% of the population, and the incidence can increase to 18-35% in people with psychological disturbances or learning or behavioural problems. Children with behavioural issues, ADHD, and autism have been found to have pyrrole disorder in association with high levels of oxidative stress... (Pyrrole disorder can) bind several nutrient cofactors, in particular vitamin B6 and zinc, essentially rendering them unavailable for use by the body. B6 and zinc are critical for digestion, immune function, cognition, and emotion, and chronic depletion can have serious consequences on wellbeing."[1]

This undoubtedly had a big effect on my state of mind as pyroluria (another name for it) has been found to be commonly associated with depression and anxiety (something worth checking for yourself if you haven't already done so). I now notice the difference if I stop taking my nutritionals. As an aside, this condition isn't recognised by many mainstream doctors. When I regularly take my nutrition, I feel fine. I suspect that more than anything, it is

---

[1] https://www.fxmedicine.com.au/blog-post/pyrrole-disorder-identification-and-treatment

probably associated with the lack of real nutrition in most food nowdays, as I discussed above.

The children and my husband felt remarkably better using all these products – skin rashes left, energy levels boosted, and general illness became extremely rare as we boosted our natural immunity. I also had psoriasis, which started to clear. When on anti-depressants, I found I was constantly bruised and having weird skin issues. These all started to recede.

When you look into it and do your own research, common products we use every day are full of nasties – not just cleaning products but toothpaste, shampoo, soap, and even baby products. These go into our body, onto our skin, and we digest them. This can affect our organs, our skin, our eyes, and our microbiome and gut health, ultimately affecting our mental health as everything is connected. Even many off-the-shelf processed foods are laden with chemicals.

So we started nourishing our bodies and taking more care with what we ate and how we looked after ourselves. We were lucky, being on the land, that we grew our own veggies and knew what was going into them and our meat supply. We had beautiful, clear artesian water. However, not everyone can obtain or afford to eat organically or have lovely, fresh water, so nutrition is definitely necessary.

We were also big smokers at the time, which I now know also depletes your body – took mainstream a long time to announce that, and they tried to hide it for an even longer time. Eventually we were able to kick that unhelpful

habit – another transformation. I have to admit, we do like to indulge in a drink, so we're still working on that one! However, the changes we have implemented mean we can be a bit naughty now and then. As I said in the intro, I am definitely not perfect!

What we also realised was that the chemicals we were using on the farm were also affecting our health significantly – poisons, herbicides, sheep dips – so we changed those processes too and helped our bodies detox.

Free, Simple, Nourishing Things We Can Do Every Day

Some basic things that are nourishing, simple, and free that we often forget about are:

- Water: Water is essential for our body, especially natural, filtered water without additives such as chlorine and fluoride. Our body is approximately 70% water, and everyone requires at least 2L or more of drinking water a day to function properly. This can definitely affect our brain function and overall health. What is your water intake? If you are in town or have tank water, is your water filtered?

- Breath: How do you breathe? Slow, deep breathing brings in our life force. Most people are not breathing or even standing properly to enable them to take in life force. How is your posture – do you hold your head up? I realised I often held my breath and spent a good deal of the day looking down, not up. Holding your head up not only opens your rib cage and lungs but

also affects the way you look at things. We cannot live without breath; it is an essential pillar of our health, and we need to focus on this. Shallow breathing wreaks havoc on our health. The way you breathe indicates your emotional state. If you notice your breath, it will immediately change. You can slowly and intentionally breathe through resistance, anxiety, and upset.

- Sleep: How is your sleep? What time do you go to bed? Do you have a ritual? Do you put your phone away from your head? Is your head racing at 100 miles an hour when you get to bed? There are many things we can do to help sleep. Have you checked your melatonin levels? Do you get enough magnesium? We find it helpful to sometimes go to bed with brainwave audios that help to change our states of consciousness.

- Grounding, Nature, and the Sun: Going out in nature, standing on the ground with your shoes off, connecting with the Earth, and being in the sun are all so important for your health on all levels. The importance of the sun on our skin and taken in through our eyes cannot be overestimated. I have heard some wonderful doctors speak about how much this can affect our wellbeing. The average person is now covering up too much and missing out on vitamin D3, which has so many health benefits, especially for natural immunity and warding off harmful diseases.

- Exercise that resonates with you: I always hated exercise until I found something I love that resonates with me – Qi Gong – an ancient energy practice that connects you to your life force. I now practise Qi Gong

regularly. Movement can help to remove stagnation, tension, pain, and discomfort, and it can release old energy from your body. Can you find an exercise that you enjoy, especially one where you can be in nature and that you can feel comfortable doing? Dancing is a great one for many people. Shaking your body is also great for releasing stagnant energy – notice how kids and animals do this constantly and seem to reset themselves. I love to start my day with some sort of foundation of relaxation. Do what works for you.

- Relaxation and Meditation: How often do you just relax and be with yourself while quieting your mind? I used to always be running around like a chook with my head cut off, thinking of endless things that HAD to be done. Often running out of energy, and then nothing got done. Nourish your soul by connecting within. Even if it is just to sit peacefully with a cup of tea that you made with awareness. Or if your life is hectic, take a bit of a longer shower and allow the water to cleanse and clear your energy. Having a soak in the tub is also a great way to relax and replenish yourself.

- Laughter and Fun: Do things that bring you joy and get you laughing again. Loosen up. Watch a silly cartoon, play like you did as a child, or better still, with a child. Be creative, dance, sing, or put on music you love. Do whatever you can to bring a spark of joy and laughter into your day. Lay on the grass and look at the clouds or stars.

I have a huge list of different things we can do to nourish ourselves; however, that is another book or perhaps a course in itself – my next goal!

One of the most bizarre things during the pandemic was the fact that people were unable to do a lot of these things that nourish them. Their breathing was masked, and they were unable to be in the sun or connect with others, which is also important. I think this shows that government and big pharma don't want you to be well, they put fear over facts. It appears they want people to rely on medications and vaccinations rather than natural immunity, which all these things build. Doctors were silenced and unable to speak out without repercussions. Media was paid to promote the government line. Medical schools and studies are mostly funded by the big pharmaceutical and vaccine-producing companies, and it seems many doctors and government bureaucrats received handbacks for promoting these things... Something to research and consider! It also doesn't seem the interactions of pharmaceuticals and other medical interventions taken together are looked into often enough by most of the mainstream medical professionals (holistic doctors and therapists exempted).

As I mentioned earlier, it is not your fault if you didn't realise other possibilities existed and if you believed what you were told by mainstream medicine and general opinion. The funny thing is when I questioned the doctors about being able to cure my depression myself and them not having told me it was possible, they said, "Oh we know it is possible to cure depression via natural methods, but no one wants to take that road; it is too slow, and it won't last. There is no point in even mentioning it."

Well I am here to encourage you that even though in the short-term it is slower than popping meds every day, in the long-term, it is ultimately more rewarding and brings

you far greater love, joy, health, and reasons for living. You can transform and change your life for the better.

I hear stories of doctors handing out meds to anyone who feels a bit down. I see people all around me who think meds are the only way. I want you to know this is not the case; you have choices, you are not stuck, you are NOT your label, and you can become self-responsible and feel better within yourself. I want to disrupt and dislodge the hold of big pharma.

Nourish Your Mind and Release Your Poor Me Story

The chemical-free household products led me to network marketing, where I took part in the training, which was awesome. I do feel like network marketing gets a bad wrap – even though I was never really successful with the business side, I do know many people that have done extremely well. Apart from being able to help others as well as yourself with the products, the personal development is incredible nourishment for the mind – encouraging you to believe in yourself. I loved this.

This gave me another big clue to finding myself, "Love what you do, and do what you love" (Dr John Demartini). Through personal development, I found myself awakening to endless possibilities. Little by little, I started realising how, what, why, and when I became depressed. I started identifying some of the triggers and how I could shift my response. I couldn't get enough of books, programmes, and courses that helped me to expand and grow. I was

drawn to anything that could transform the way I thought and what was possible for my life and my family.

One of my favourite exercises that had a profound effect early in my new life was to take whatever "poor me" story I had going on in my head and write it out, speak it out, until it became boring and mundane. This serves to dissolve and transform the "charge" around the experience. Remember, we are energy, and it is like you are plugged into an electrical socket when your e-motions (energy in motion) run wild. As my friend, Jen Jeffries often says "No story, no problem" – I have discovered this is very true.

If you are going to do this, you have to be gentle on yourself though, and ensure you don't wallow in the story. Also, don't start with anything too traumatic, start with little things. For example, Mary Bloggs doesn't like me, and I am so sick of the way she talks to me. She makes me so mad, etc., etc. Self-talk like this is being powerless, you are making yourself co-dependent on someone else's behaviour. No one else can really "make" you feel anything, it is all going on inside you.

By writing it out and reading it aloud, you can realise it is "just a story" and view it from a different perspective, an out-of-body or helicopter perspective. By doing this, I found I could take what I needed to learn from the experience and make peace with it and myself. I could acknowledge, connect with, and accept myself, the experience and my feelings about it rather than push it away. This also helps to quieten the ego, the little voice that always wants to be right or tells you to ignore things as it tries to keep you 'safe'.

Discovering Yourself and Your Points of View to Connect with Your Soul

I began to realise that my self-esteem was non-existent. In fact, I hated myself, and I was totally addicted to feeling sorry for myself. How could I nourish myself when I didn't care about me? How could I nourish my husband or children when I had nothing to give? It began to register in my closed-off self that I needed to change dramatically, and this was frightening but necessary. I spent a lot of time doing exercises and letting things out. It was a slow process but a necessary one if I was to become who I needed to be for myself and others.

I started discovering myself and what I loved. I started shifting my points of view, my perceptions of myself and others. I started to realise we are all energy and all souls here to experience life in different ways. I learnt to heal and transform my thoughts, feelings, words, and actions. To be able to go within and connect with my soul and spirit, my true self. To find my I AM. I learnt to respond rather than react.

Something else that had a huge effect on the way I talked to myself and others was an experiment done with water by a Japanese Scientist, Dr Masaru Emoto. Put very basically, Dr Emoto found that the molecular structure of water transforms when it is exposed to human words, thoughts, sounds, and intentions. Basically what he found was that water exposed to loving, kind, and compassionate human intention resulted in beautiful physical molecular formations in the water that looked like snowflakes. Water exposed to fearful and angry human intentions resulted in disconnected, disfigured, 'ugly' formations.

Now remember we are at least 70% water – so the way we talk or think to ourselves is going to affect us – or if you talk to others that way, it will also affect them! I was often angry and yelling at my family for no reason. It began to dawn on me what I was doing. Speak nastily to yourself, and your body will vibrate in accordance with those thoughts and burst out from within you to others (like an orange being squeezed or a burst pipe). If you speak lovingly, your body will radiate love to yourself and others. Quite a sobering thought, isn't it? I know it isn't always possible as we are human; however, it's something to keep in mind.

Heavy Metals, Your Gut and Detoxing

Once feeling better and learning that there was more natural help out there, I went to a naturopath who found that I had high toxic heavy metal levels in my body. So we did further work with antioxidants, herbs and oils, and other nutrition to detox. I also realised the meds were affecting my gut and overall health as well. Your gut is connected to your brain and affects your state of mind. This experience was wonderful as it introduced me to another level of natural healing that I have now embraced as a healer myself. I reconnected with the same naturopath a few years ago to help me grow further and to boost my nutrition even more. It seems nothing is by chance and everything is connected.

I constantly follow my intuition now, and if I feel drawn to something, I do it. Over 10 years ago I was receiving treatment from a chiropractor who also used kinesiology. This is a form of biofeedback from your body to indicate imbalances in the body and what might be causing those imbalances. His treatments helped me immensely,

and I was able to release a lot of things I hadn't yet realised I was holding onto or was blocking. I found this so amazing and so healing for me that I decided to study this modality professionally myself. In doing so, I found an amazing teacher who has become a great friend and has mentored me ever since. Another naturopath friend, who I visited to help me detox after a setback, set me on a path to seeking further healing and to meeting an amazing man who encouraged me to become an energy healer and all I could be. I am so grateful for following my intuition in seeking help. I feel blessed that my illness has led me to meet some incredible and inspiring people in my life.

I found kinesiology to be quite miraculous because you can simply ask your body – or someone else's – what is causing the imbalance, and you are directed to what you or they might need. You can also do surrogate healings for children and distance healing (a real passion of mine, which I will tell you more about at the end of this book). You can find answers to anything, especially how, why, what, and when an issue occurred. For example, was it physical, mental, spiritual (energetic), or chemical? Through this, you can realise the cause of the issue and change your vibration and, therefore, your results in life. With intention and intuition, I can now tune into myself and ask, "What do I need?" I can now also do this with energy healing.

Mercury Poisoning and Teeth

It was via a kinesiology treatment in class that I discovered I had a mercury issue which turned out to be mercury poisoning. I was able to seek appropriate help from a holistic dentist. No wonder I was having problems remembering things and having some other very weird

health issues! It is not a nice experience. However, via this incident, I learnt how important our teeth are to our health. I had a badly infected tooth that I didn't know about, and I felt much better after its safe removal.

Standard dental practices are not generally helping us as we would assume. Root canals can cause severe issues with your health, as can amalgam fillings (which contain mercury), especially if not removed properly. Braces may be required because children are actually not breathing properly or have poor posture, which affects the way their teeth form. Fluoride that goes into the water and that most dentists use can actually calcify and close down your pineal gland. Not only can this affect your sleep and your hormones – which can lead to depression and headaches – but the pineal gland plays a major role in our spiritual development and communication within. Something that is truly important to our wellbeing. It seems to me that perhaps our government or the powers that be are trying to dumb us down in as many ways as possible, one way being putting fluoride into the water. I now take everything they say with a grain of salt and use my discernment and true knowing about whether these things they advocate are nourishing for my family and me, or not!

Your Home, Your Body, Electromagnetic Fields and Other Imbalances

It is also a good idea to be mindful of EMFs (electromagnetic fields) from your phone, wifi, landlines, etc., as these can play havoc with your body and your mental health. Scientists have found that the heart itself has an EMF of

approximately 3 feet,[2] so other EMFs coming into your heart space are going to affect your heart and your mental health.

Apart from these things, there are soooo many physical and chemical things that can also affect us, such as mould, parasites, candida, processed foods, hormones injected into our food as well as our own hormone imbalances, neurotransmitters being disrupted (these are chemical substances in the nerve cell that either stimulate or inhibit the next nerve call response. Because of their effect on our nervous system they are able to affect the whole body's response.) Structural problems especially cranial issues can also effect us. Not to mention what is on the mental and spiritual side! That is why it is great to be able to ask your body what might actually be causing some of your issues and drill down to what is immediately needed. This can take years off visits to psychiatrists and psychologists!

Studying kinesiology and working with others on a daily basis, I was able to really heal a lot of past trauma. I then found that about 95% of my healing experience, and that of my clients, related to energy healing, so that has become my passion. I have realised the enormity of the fact that we really are all energy and all connected. Once we can reset our energy and truly connect with love and our light within, we truly can transform ourselves (and others) and realise that is why we are here.

----

[2] https://www.heartmath.org/research/science-of-the-heart/energetic-communication/

Follow-Up Exercises – What Can You Implement or Change?

- Write in your journal the things you might want to look at and consider, implement, and change or follow up on.

- What can you do every day that might change or influence your overall health, lifestyle, and the way you feel?

- Some basic things to start looking at and considering their possible effects on you and your family are: (mind you, the list is really endless)
  - Water quality and amount of water you're drinking
  - Food quality and what is sprayed on it before, during and after growing, injected into it, genetic modification, glue etc
  - Sleep quality and the amount of sleep you get
  - Nutrition or lack of nutrition
  - Exercise or lack of exercise
  - How you breathe
  - Your posture
  - Relaxation and meditation
  - Grounding and energetic protection
  - Laughter and fun
  - Household products
  - Chemicals inside and out
  - Heavy metals
  - Detoxing
  - Your dental health

- ○ EMFs
- ○ Your home in general
- ○ Mould
- ○ Parasites, candida, hormones
- ○ Medications and vaccinations

- How do you nourish your body, mind, spirit, and soul, and how do you connect within?

- What stories do you tell yourself about your life? If they are not nourishing, then write out and read aloud (without judgement) a story or two till you are sick of it – it will help you become aware of what you are saying to yourself. For example, "The other day someone cut me off while I was in the middle of talking, and it was just plain rude. No one ever listens to me". You can then move onto bigger ones!

- Are you doing what you love? If not, why not? (This might be another story!)

- How do you speak to yourself and your body? Would you speak to someone else that way?

"Love is the capacity to take care, to protect, to nourish."

—Thich Nhat Hanh

Let's Get Real – What is Your "Real-ationship" with Yourself and Others?

"Be who you are and say what you feel, because those who mind don't matter and those who matter don't mind."

—Dr. Seuss

Being YOU

Once I had started to improve my health, I knew that in order to feel differently, I needed to think differently about myself. Change was necessary. This was scary. I re-alised I had spent a lot of time trying to control and focus on others so as to take the spotlight off myself. Realisation is about finding you and **being you** – letting go of the old conditioning that keeps you stuck in a charade, masking who you really are. When you are able to connect within to the real you and REALise who you really are, you will truly understand your internal power.

To change our habit and our addiction to BE-ing depressed, we need to realise when we are acting unconsciously –

reacting to people, places, events, and situations. You are a human be-ing in a state; this state can be changed when you realise you can be whoever you want. Think of yourself as an actor. Stop allowing life to do you rather than you doing life. Reclaim yourself. We CAN end this endless battle inside ourselves. There is no need to run, fix, hide, or be someone you are not. We merely need to observe what is going on. Uproot your resistance to facing fear – stop running, and if triggered, say, "That's not who I am". What is the trigger trying to show you, tell you? Stop, breathe, check within, ground yourself, and listen.

Have you really looked at your self-worth? How do you feel about yourself and others? I know I thought very little of myself. I was stuck in my role and way of thinking from back as a child, and I kept reacting like a child. I would react like a child rather than respond as an adult. For example, if my husband said something I didn't agree with or I didn't like, I would throw a tanty or burst out crying. That would then result in an argument with him going into his inner child and storming off stamping his feet, and me going into endless sobbing, hiding myself in resentment with a loop of thoughts about feeling sorry for myself, how I was right, and he was just plain mean (much like I had felt as a child or teenager with my parents)!

I thought the whole world was against me – everyone wanted to hurt me. I continually compared myself to others and was always worried about how people saw me. Always berating myself for not being as clever, articulate, funny, or pretty as others and for not living up to others' perceived expectations. I was really quite self-absorbed and self-indulgent in a critical, opinionated, and controlling way

with no self-love at all. I lived a mask of trying to look like the person I thought I wasn't – fun, successful, powerful.

I was constantly apologising for being me. My self-confidence was at zero. Even now writing this book, I can feel the old lack of self-confidence bubbling up. That little voice in my head saying, "Who on Earth is going to want to read what you are writing? There are so many great writers out there with so much knowledge – what do you really have to offer? Why are you even bothering?" So I have to take that little voice in hand and say, "Thank you for that; however, I have walked my talk, done the hard yards in life, and know I have something to offer others, so I am going to give this a whirl! Nothing ventured, nothing gained, and we are actually having fun doing this!"

We are learning to love all of who we are so we can give to ourselves and naturally give to others. This giving then comes from the real self, not the false, masked self.

Talk to Your Inner Self to Release Trauma

Inner child work is amazing for realising how you are stuck reacting as you did when you were a child. Once you start connecting with yourself, you are able to talk to your body and feel the stuck emotions. Ask yourself, "When did this happen before, and what age were you? What was going on, who was there? It took me quite a while to connect like this and get any answers, I guess because I had been so disconnected from myself. It then feels amazing to have this child open up to you and to be able to soothe your child. So much of what happens to us comes from our past and especially our first seven years.

I discovered that I felt myself a victim, unloved, unwanted, not good enough, somehow bad or flawed, and defective in some way. I had been traumatised when I was young, and rather than releasing this trauma, I became this trauma. I found via sessions with a kinesiologist that there was a large trauma I had suppressed deep within and didn't even remember until it came up and out of my mouth. Often there are things we cannot face at the time, and we bury them deep within our psyche and cover them up. I was able to work through this and come to peace with it. I then understood why I was the way I was in my teenage years and early 20s. I didn't value myself – thought I was flawed and a failure. And as a result of my experience, I drank to excess and gave myself away, trying to feel and find love and be wanted.

Everyone experiences trauma in different ways. I have heard some horrific stories of what happened to people – some are able to cope emotionally, and others not. Like me, some hide it and suppress what happened as they have been unable to deal with it. Some people who have had quite sheltered lives are still traumatised by small issues. As I said, we are all different; however, in almost everyone, I still see the same patterns of somehow thinking we are not enough or flawed in some way.

When traumatised at a young age, it can affect our brain development. We become ashamed of who and what we are as a person. We become stuck in our point of view, perception, and belief of what happened, that is, that we were rejected, unloved, unworthy. Instead of living in the now and responding accordingly when an event occurs, we unconsciously go back in time and associate those

feelings we felt in the past with what is happening in the now, and we react as we would have as a child.

I also realised I was a people-pleaser trying to make others happy, trying to be enough for them, wanting to look special in their eyes, trying to receive their love. My first memory of this came from when I was about five, working on our passionfruit farm. We had a contest for who could build passionfruit boxes the fastest, and I won. I received so much attention and praise. It is still talked about! I remember feeling so proud. I now realise my thinking was that if I do what people want, I will get their praise and attention, and if I try really hard, be as fast as I can, and follow their instructions, they will love me. I was very often nice to others yet exploding within or at my family (where we often feel safe to express our true self).

Apart from wanting to please and follow others' instructions, I also learnt to go hard and fast as my approach to a lot of my life, which often didn't serve me. I never learnt when to pull up and take a rest for me, to integrate and acknowledge what I was doing, had learnt or achieved rather than going till I virtually collapsed.

Not being able to say "no" to things I really didn't want to do and going along with the crowd got me in a lot of trouble throughout my life. In my book "Lessons from a Conman", I write about our experience when we lost all our money to a conman. This involved me not being able to say "no" to him, thinking I didn't know enough, wanting to please him as I perceived he was more knowledgeable and powerful, and wanting to go along with the crowd. I was not trying to please myself. I did things out of obligation and wanting to

look good rather than out of love and appreciation for the knowledge I already had. In my eyes, I had to try and be perfect to be loved, and this also meant I did what others wanted or what I thought they wanted rather than listen to myself. I was obsessed with trying to look perfect and prove myself on the outside while screaming and being a total mess on the inside.

Are You Being a Drama Queen?

I was a drama queen, everything was a big deal – my life was a soap opera. I would blow little things all out of proportion to make them into big, important, dramatic stories. I took everything personally. A simple example of this would be: if my husband happened to not be listening to something I said and I had to repeat it, I would say things to him like, "You never listen to me anyway, you obviously don't love me at all," and I would storm off or start crying. I would blame problems on outside drama or others rather than my own choices.

If I made a mistake or was unable to go somewhere or do something I was supposed to do, it was due to some elaborate story seemingly out of my control. I subconsciously thought my actions demanded attention and that I would be noticed (like a Queen). I often used the words always, never, everything – this is drama queen stuff – the all or nothing – there is only black or white – no in between – a very limited view of life. I was always busy trying to gain attention to feel and look important and needed. This also resulted in me being a bit of a gossip. It is so easy to talk about and judge others rather than face yourself. I think this behaviour helps build your identity as a

drama queen and an authority as to what is going on with others and what they are doing or not doing.

There wasn't much "being" a powerful me or thinking for myself, or giving myself the attention I needed rather than trying to demand it from others. If you're "always" at the centre of a drama, what are you doing to create this situation? Are you evoking attention or excitement? Are you trying to manipulate others or controlling a situation? Are there self-destructive behaviours involved? Do you talk about or judge others? Also, in my writing, do you see all the "trying" in the words above rather than "being"? It is great to observe yourself, become conscious, and listen to what you are saying to people or telling yourself. Once you become aware in this way, you will be astonished to find that most of the dramas actually go away.

I hid my true self to hide from feeling pain, from being abandoned, unwanted, or laughed at. I put up a façade, so no one would see who I really was. All the while my shame, guilt, and embarrassment at not being perfect, funny, or beautiful made me smaller and smaller and more disconnected from myself. By not thinking I was perfect, I would strive for perfectionism. I have now found that striving is unbelievably exhausting – it is much easier to get in the flow.

I found I was also a rebel. As I didn't want to be hurt, I had a bit of an "up yours" attitude and wanted to do things to intentionally hurt others in an attempt to hide my own pain. I was great at playing the victim by blaming others for my pain and not taking responsibility for myself. I now realise this rebel is inquisitive and likes to push the boundaries,

which I can now do in a healthy way. Once you come to terms with the not-so-good, the bad, and the ugly parts of yourself, what are termed your shadow-self, you can appreciate their roles in a more positive way.

The False Self Behind the Mask

When working through my pain, I realised that as an adult, I was still repeating the same feelings and behaviours I had as a child. Seeing myself as insecure, injured, victimised, and a bad person who would never know enough or be good enough. I also realised I had become a false self – empty – self-absorbed – constantly worrying about what everyone else thought of me so that I couldn't hear my voice within. I was more worried about trying to fit in and be like everyone else and be accepted rather than be my unique self. I was always putting what everyone else wanted before my own needs and then resenting them for it rather than realising that it had been my choice to ignore myself. I was definitely not listening to myself, something I was constantly accusing others of, "you never listen to me".

We all have a responsibility to ourselves and to others to make our lives worth living, so shed your skin, the old mask you have been wearing, and remember who you are. Your inner world is the cause of your despair, and the outer world is merely the effect – your reflection, if you will. We think we are hiding behind these masks we wear and that no one can see who we really are. In actual fact, people see straight through the mask and see you exactly as you see yourself. Nothing is ever about what someone else is doing or not doing; it is always about what is going on inside you. To reach the gold, you have to find what is

hidden inside you and transform it by recognising it and finding out how you can acknowledge and make peace with that part of yourself. I also needed to find a way to put myself first while still being a decent human being and not becoming even more selfish and self-centred.

I have learnt it is easy to blame the messenger when things go wrong; however, it is always about you – you are the messenger. I was always feeling there was something wrong with me – I often felt judged or rejected. However, this was me judging and rejecting myself. Becoming conscious of this negative self-talk and this self-blame is freedom – that is the gold, as once you see it, you can let it go and transform it into words of love or even just encouragement to start with.

What Happened and What Did You Make it Mean?

What happened to you that you haven't dealt with – what did you make it mean? Kinesiology and other energy work are great in that it enables us to ask and find the answers to these questions. Undealt with trauma in our body and mind leads to pain, hardness, restriction, and constriction. We need to release this gently. It is not so much about what happened to you but what happened inside you when the event occurred. At that point, people generally separate from themselves and disconnect from others in order to survive and cope. It then becomes difficult to be in the present moment as you are stuck in the past and keep reacting to and recreating that past in the now. Rather than beat yourself up, can you ask yourself what you learnt from the experience? When we discover the lessons,

we can begin to forgive and feel grateful and have better, more fulfilling connections with others.

If you are not allowed to be yourself by your parents, teachers, and those who are influential around you, or if you are controlled too much, this can lead to suppression of your true self. This can ignite different personalities or archetypes within you, such as the rebel, the self-saboteur, the victim, the wounded child, or the abandoned child. This is where you will strive to please others to be accepted by them, and then you start on the comparison treadmill. Were you or are you still overburdened and overwhelmed with responsibilities and trying to fit someone else's idea of who you should be? I felt I was.

Can you allow yourself to feel and express your pain so that you can move on? Be careful to do it without staying in that pain for too long! Can you find the magic and possibilities that you may have lost from childhood? You need to be vigilant with what you are saying to yourself, what you believe, feel, hear, or see within. Your mind is hardwired to resist anything unfamiliar, and it will want to run back to your old ways. However, know that if you consistently change the way you look at things, the things you look at will change.

I find a great way to see how you are going is to use others as mirrors. If your relationships aren't changing, then you are probably stuck. If someone close triggers feelings in you, then go back to when you first remember feeling that emotion, and find out what was going on then. And keep going back until you get to the source and are no longer triggered.

"It is not the mountain we conquer but ourselves."
—*Edmund Hillary*

Be the Witness and Acknowledge

If you can witness and acknowledge how, what, why, and when you became depressed or where your self-criticism and self-loathing comes from, this is a major step in healing and transforming. Whatever you are thinking or feeling is not in alignment with your Higher Self. By acknowledging and transforming these feelings, you can then create a new you – the you you always were before you moulded yourself to fit everyone else. You can build your confidence in yourself and your abilities, and you can become victorious.

All of this is a work in progress – a remembering and a becoming – we can all slip up at times, and it is getting back up again that makes the difference. Even after I think I have worked through all my issues, little things still pop up at times for me to work on. I think that if we were perfect we would no longer need to be here. We are all constantly evolving, so it is important to go easy on yourself. Remember where you have come from and how far you have come.

I will give you an example from how I was feeling and the thoughts that were going through my head before deciding to finally write this book (which I have had in my heart for some time now). This is a post I wrote on my business page only a couple of months ago. By the way, in my state when writing, I had blurted out a lot of the things I describe as feelings below, but most of them are not feelings; they are beliefs which cause you to feel sad! So it

takes a while to be able to recognise exactly what you are doing. Sometimes you have to step back for a bit.

"I had a crap day yesterday. 💩

I woke up and did my normal spiritual practices, which generally help keep me in line. I was feeling on Cloud 9 ☁️ *believing I could do anything, and then, whack!* ⚡😨😳

I was brought back down to Earth with a reminder of what I haven't achieved, haven't done. After a lot of tears, upset, and retreating back into myself, I began thinking, "What's the point? Why bother even trying? 😰 *Maybe I should just pack everything up and just end it all, or do I continue my old routine of going through the motions, appearing happy when I am shrivelling inside because I am not following my soul's yearning, knowing what I am supposed to be doing in this life?* 🙃

I then remembered a time early in primary school – getting that same "whack" – although that whack was a physical one with the ruler over my knuckles. 📏 *A reminder that I was not good enough, not performing as I should be.* 😠 *Mrs Topp was a cruel teacher, a hard, bitter woman – constantly rapping you over the knuckles or whacking you across the head. The elders in my family thought she was the bee's knees producing great results – to me she was evil incarnate.* 👹 *However, it is important to remember not to shoot the messenger – who knows what she went through in her life, and she was just trying to wake me up and get me to "perform" in obviously the only way she knew how.*

So I realised at 57 I am still repeating those same feelings and behaviours that Mrs Topp helped instil in me when someone points out my failures – what I haven't done or haven't done properly. The feelings of – why bother, what's the point, the injustice, insecurity, fear, sadness, lack of confidence, not feeling good enough, feeling victimised – are like a physical attack. I have already done a lot of work on these memories, so I guess this is hopefully the last realisation of that experience, and I can now transform it and the associated emotions!

To escape these feelings (which I didn't really realise I had till now), I normally just unconsciously push them down and then sabotage myself by crying, drinking, retreating, sulking, rebelling, getting angry, being depressed, and shutting myself off from the world – (which I did yesterday and this morning) without realising why.

Now that I recognise these feelings and what I am doing, I can acknowledge them and feel them instead of repressing them, so they can magically transform. However this time, I seem stuck in the feelings, so I know there are other processes I need to do to help.

To do this I worked on myself as I would a client, going through my lists of what I need to heal this issue and associated blockages. I feel a huge weight has lifted off my shoulders.

Nothing is ever about what someone else is doing or not doing – it is always about what is going on inside you. To reach the gold, you have to find what is going on inside and transform it by recognising it and finding out how

you can acknowledge and make peace with that part of yourself. 

I have learnt it is easy to blame the messenger; however, it is always about you, and you are the messenger – in my case, it was my inner child trying to bring things to my attention that felt unacknowledged or undealt with from the past.. I believe we try or bother for the deep yearning inside us to be and do our something special in this world. When we feel knocked down, it is easy to just shut ourselves off – say, "Why bother? What's the point? It is just all too hard", and retreat back into our shell. It is easier to do that and say, "Well I tried, but it didn't work because of x,y,z", or to not even try at all, and that way, you don't need to be hurt. However, I know it is worth it because the feeling of giving something your soul is yearning for a go is far more rewarding than not doing anything."

RAIN Down on Strong Emotions With Love Technique

You can probably see in my post above all the self-judgement I had going on, as well as limited beliefs. Fear and judgement cannot live in the same place as love and power. One of my techniques I use to help myself not get too lost is what I call RAIN – the rain of love can help wash away the pain.

• Recognise strong emotions as they occur.

• Acknowledge and allow the emotion – stop resisting the present moment.

- Investigate – bring self-analysis to the moment – ask: What am I really upset about, and how could I think differently?

- Non-identify and release judgement – this serves to deflate and minimise the connection between your self-worth and the situation. This increases understanding that the emotion is not you but represents a moment in time and a situation. Is it even an emotion, or is it a belief that is causing me to feel this emotion?

- Love – Bring love into the moment. Let the beliefs go, and allow the emotion (energy in motion) to release by breathing it out, allowing the storm to pass and to be transformed and replaced with love and a sense of peace. Think about how you really want to feel, who you want to be.

I hope you find that useful. There are so many tools and techniques we can use to help us transform and release to find our inner gold.

How Do You Look After You?

Getting real with yourself also means looking after yourself. Learning to truly love and appreciate yourself. How are your appearance, clothes, and hair? Take a good look at this, as it is a reflection of how you see yourself and whether you take pride in you. I used to slouch around in old worn clothes, not feeling I deserved lovely clothes or feeling that people would judge me as being "up myself" if I took too much care.

Do you have time for yourself, and do you do things just for you, just for the fun or creativity of it? I used to think this was "wasting time" – I was not worth it and had to keep busy, or at least the appearance of it as that made me seem important. Do you savour your relationships and make them special and fun, especially the relationship with yourself and your immediate family?

How is your home environment? Do you take care of your home, nourish it, keep it clean, and clear out clutter? Being in an uncared-for environment as well as body can also affect our moods.

Journalling is great for realising what you are thinking – for writing out angry thoughts. Or even speak them out, yell them into a pillow. All those harsh thoughts and words are better out where they can be transformed rather than held in and ignored where they will continue to cause more pain and suffering.

Sometimes we can be like a kinked hose about to burst under pressure. We are holding onto, constricting, and constraining ourselves, strangling ourselves, and stopping the true us from coming out. We are not allowing ourselves to flow or for love to come through, and this can sometimes result in an explosion of pent-up emotion. When we are able to journal and reflect on ourselves, this eases the pressure and unkinks the hose. What do you like and dislike about yourself and others? Write this out. This can be great to start to see your beliefs and judgements, which we will work on next.

Follow-up Exercises – Question Everything and Unkink That Hose

If you can witness and acknowledge how, what, why, and when you became depressed or where your self-criticism and self-loathing comes from, this is a major step in healing and transforming.

- Is there some massive trauma from your past that you're still experiencing and reacting to now? Do you need help with solving this? If so, please stop and seek help, and don't try to do this on your own. This is not a race, and you need to take care of yourself first and foremost.

- Can you list any times you can remember when you realise you have acted unconsciously –reacting rather than responding to people, places, events, and situations?

- In your present life, what do you feel triggers you or causes you to react to a situation in an unconscious way? In other words, what triggers you into reactions such as rage, playing the victim, being the drama queen, pleasing others, or bursting into tears?

- What are these triggers trying to show you and tell you?

- What comes up for you when you talk to your inner child?

- Connect with yourself, talk to your body, and feel the stuck emotions. Gently invite your body to tell you when this feeling was there first. What was your age? What was going on? Who was there?

- Can you see what you are unconsciously creating by acting in certain ways? For example, drama queens unconsciously create, manifest, and draw drama into their lives.

- If you're "always" at the centre of a drama, what are you doing to create this situation? Are you evoking attention and excitement, or are you unknowingly attempting to manipulate or control others or a situation? Are there any self-destructive behaviours involved?

- Do you blame problems on outside drama or others rather than your own choices?

- Do you take things personally when perhaps they weren't meant that way or directed at you. Can you ask yourself if this is how you truly feel about yourself when in fact it has nothing to do with you?

- Are you often talking about or judging others? Can you become more aware of this and begin to change these habits?

- What masks do you wear in your life? What would it take to remove them and be more fully yourself?

- What are the roles of your "shadow-self" – the parts you think are bad or unworthy? Are there parts of

you that you continually don't want to acknowledge? Can you find and speak to these parts with love and acknowledge how they have been trying to protect you? For example, the victim who might be trying to hide and protect you from what it sees as further hurt can become the victorious by allowing you to be your true self and stand up for yourself.

- What happened to you that you haven't dealt with – what did you make it mean? We need to release this gently. It is not so much about what happened to you but **what happened inside you** when the event occurred. Can you ask yourself what you learnt from the experience?

- Are you on the comparison treadmill? Do you constantly compare yourself with others? Can you acknowledge how amazing you are within yourself and that everyone is different? We all have different qualities to bring to the world.

- Were you or are you still overburdened and overwhelmed with responsibilities, and are you trying to fit someone else's idea of who you should be?

- Who are you BEING? Who do you think is the real you? What are your qualities that you are proud of and would like to grow? Write it out, and begin to interact with this person.

- Have you really looked at your self-worth –how do you feel within yourself? What is your relationship with yourself? What do you like and dislike? How are your appearance, clothes, and hair?

- Do you have time for yourself, and do you do things just for you, just for the fun or creativity of it?

- How is your home environment? Do you take care of your home, nourish it, keep it clean, and keep it clear of clutter and things you no longer need? This can sometimes represent our holding onto our past unnecessarily.

- How do you feel about your relationship with others?

- Do you savour your relationships and make them special and fun, especially the relationship with yourself and your immediate family?

- Now that you are more conscious of your negative self-talk and self-blame, can you let it go and transform it into words of love or even just encouragement to start with? What have you been telling yourself, and what might you tell yourself instead?

- Can you allow yourself to feel and express your pain so that you can move on? Be careful to do it without staying in that pain for too long! Can you find the magic and possibilities that you may have lost from childhood?

"It's not who you are that holds you back, it's who you think you're not."

— *Hanoch McCarty*

Chapter 5

Uproot Those Beliefs and Judgements – Allowing and Trusting Yourself

"I am not what happened to me. I am what I choose to become."

—Carl Jung

The sun of us cannot shine out if it hits old negative or limiting beliefs. It is time to find and uproot your limiting beliefs and judgements, which will then allow new empowering ones to come into being. Judgement and criticism of any kind, especially self-criticism, blocks our heart and stops us from being all we can be. By now in the process, you will have observed yourself, your memories, your self-talk, some of your pain, your triggers, and some of your reactions. You will also have identified where you are and where it is that you want to be, giving your mind direction so that you can use it and it does not use you. Do you now know what is stopping you from being all you can be? Do you now know that some of your main obstacles are your own internal beliefs blocking you? Beliefs that think they are protecting you!

We also need to be aware of and realise how we can delete, distort, or generalise what is occurring in our life depending on our values, beliefs, filters, personal experiences, memories, attitudes, or previous decisions we have made.

What is the Story Running in Your Mind? Let Go of Resistance

As I have said previously, everyone in our lives mirrors our opinions and judgements. What is the story that runs in you when you are pushed? For example, "I am no good, no one loves me". Can you ask yourself, "Why do I have that belief or perspective? Where did it come from?" Sometimes it can take a while to even realise it is a belief and that it can absolutely be transformed. The belief that you are not good enough is just a belief, as I am sure is the idea that **no one** loves you. Something happened to you; perhaps someone yelled at you without meaning it in the moment, "You are hopeless!" Or "I hate you right now!" Or perhaps they did actually tell you you were no good and unloveable with strong meaning. For sure, people <u>shouldn't</u> talk to each other this way, but they do, so we have to work with what we have, and once again they are our mirror.

It is important to remember that this can also come from the other person's conditioning, through what has happened to them in their life and how they feel or have dealt or not dealt with things. Once you truly come to realise this, it can be empowering, and you can see the other person from a totally different light, perhaps even with compassion. From this we can perceive that others actually give us the gift of ascertaining who we really

want to be, what we believe and what we want to believe instead. This empowers us to become better people who are more resilient. It shows us what we previously believed that was untrue.

Resistance is also a biggie – what are we resisting in ourselves and in receiving from others? Often we resist the negative or our shadow selves, and we need to examine our past memories and experiences to understand why we might be reacting defensively or resisting change. In actual fact, there is no good or bad, there just is. Negative thoughts or people can be a gift in that they are often showing us something we need to work on. They are serving us as mirrors to the parts of ourselves we are not accepting or recognising. We need to break our behavioural patterns and find out what triggers them.

If we can let go of our old beliefs and create more empowering and uplifting ones, we can make peace with the past and transform our future. To do this, pull out that journal again – I would start with Mum and Dad or your main caregiver(s) and the other significant people in your life (teachers also have great influence). What did they believe about marriage, career, children, money, religion, judgements about you and who you should be, weight, appearance, education, etc.? A lot of these beliefs are generally passed down from one generation to the next without much thought as to whether they are true or not. You can also look at what you admire them for, as this helps you see both the beliefs that may not serve you and those that may indeed be principles and values you wish to uphold more.

Make sure you keep feelings or emotions distinct from beliefs. A belief can be removed from your consciousness and replaced with something more empowering. Beliefs are not set in stone; they can be eliminated and swapped out. Emotions and feelings can only be seen, observed, felt, and acknowledged. And through this acknowledgement, feelings become accepted and transform you up the scale. You cannot remove an emotion, it will always live within you. We are like a rainbow with every emotion within, and we need to balance and be aware of those emotions and not let them consume us.

My beliefs had always been that I wasn't good enough and I had to work hard to prove myself; if I did this, I would be rewarded. This is what my experience was as a child. I totally lacked self-esteem and thought I was just an embarrassment, as this had been my inner experience when I perceived people laughing at me or my parents feeling embarrassed by something I had done. I was extremely judgemental of myself and others. I don't think I even knew what the words self-love, acceptance, or nourishment were.

I also found it important to look at the times when we take things personally. Perhaps this is more about our beliefs around how we truly feel about ourselves or perceive ourselves and has nothing to do with the message being delivered by the other person. You may have unconsciously been acting in a way you yourself don't like. I generally find if you don't react to comments from others it is normally about the other person and what is going on within them or their life and not about you at all. If you do react they are just pressing your buttons so that you can see what is going on inside yourself.

Generational Beliefs and Values

In doing the work, I realised my lack of self-esteem and self-love was generational. I have found we take on different traits, good and bad, from our parents. And the beliefs we take on depend on the way WE perceive things, OUR point of view, not how they actually might be. I felt that my parents also lacked self-love to some degree, without being aware of it, and I also passed these beliefs and values down to my children.

My father is very clever, has been successful, and achieved a lot in his life. To Dad, it was very important to know everything – when he was young, he had wanted to go to University, but due to circumstances beyond his control, he was unable to at the time. He had been in boarding school all of his school life, so education and knowledge, knowing what you were talking about, were paramount. I have learnt and gained a lot from my father's influence; however, he worked so hard to constantly prove himself to others (and I believe to himself) in different ways as a provider and father, that in my eyes, I felt he didn't have much quality time for us (purely my perception). We never really discussed feelings or what was going on inside – I guess it was about being stoic. I have spent my life constantly trying to live up to Dad's standards and prove myself to him.

My mother is an exceptional artist and very creative; however, I believe she never realised her own worth and ability to take it seriously. It was always a hobby. She had been a nurse and was all about caring for others, which is a wonderful aspiration. However, to me, Mum was always

more concerned with others, not just caring about them but also concerned about how they saw her and what they thought of her, with little regard for her own feelings. These are the traits I then took on. You can only teach people what you know to be true at the time; we are all doing our best.

These are not judgements or accusations towards my parents. It was typical of their era – for me it just was, and it was all my family knew. That was how they lived and what they valued, and what I used to value too. Their focus and what they believed was the "right thing" in life was to always be worrying about others, working hard doing things for others, and worrying about what "they" thought rather than concerning yourself with how you might feel. Focusing on how you felt was seen as selfish, which is not the truth. These are wonderful values to have if done with balance, however if they become all-consuming, they can cause you to lose sight of yourself. I used to be engrossed with all my negative traits and can now recognise and acknowledge all the wonderful qualities I inherited. I am determined, tenacious, loving, and caring. I am hardworking. I always give my best and am a great businesswoman and a loyal friend, amongst other things. I have realised I am even quite funny! (still trying to convince my family of that. Lol!)

It's All About Balance

We always had to be working hard, and there is nothing wrong with that if balanced out. As with most people I met from my parents' era, they would judge anyone who didn't live up to their beliefs and standards. There was no balance or real nourishment of self. This may not even

be the actual truth, but this was my perception of how I was brought up, and these became my values and then, unfortunately, how I began to parent my children until I became aware of what I was doing. Of course my parents had some wonderful traits I also took on, but I never noticed or acknowledged these for a long time, as I was too focused on negative traits. I exaggerated what I felt even more by putting everyone else before myself, looking at others rather than focusing on me, comparing myself to them, and needing to prove myself to them in order to feel important, acknowledged, and seen rather than just BEING me and looking after myself. I was constantly apologising for who I was as I didn't see myself as worthy in their eyes.

When I first got married and moved to far Western Queensland, it was such an eye-opener for me. I hadn't really considered that people lived differently to the way I had been brought up and lived my life. It was a bit of a culture shock, and I was stuck in "My way is the right way". And, it generally wasn't since I had a distorted view of many things! Our families did have some similar beliefs, but it was tricky navigating the contrasts. My husband was not at all judgemental, well mostly not!

It wasn't until we attended some courses with people who all had varying ideas and beliefs that I started questioning my beliefs and began to understand. I realised how, as different people, our values, beliefs, and the way we each live, actually shapes our life. I acknowledged how different everyone can be, and I realised I could drop some of my limiting beliefs to then pick and choose the beliefs I wanted to follow according to my values. Those new beliefs then enabled me to change my life for the better.

So go through your own beliefs and those you see in the world around you. Now this too can be a really long list! So start with things you know will make a difference immediately. The biggies like, "I can't get anything right – I am hopeless". When we have strong beliefs, we tend to hold an energy that confirms those beliefs. So, from the belief that I was hopeless, I would continue making mistakes and attracting people and events to confirm my belief that I was hopeless.

Money ones are especially great to work on too for example, "Money doesn't grow on trees!" When you find beliefs that don't serve you, the best idea is to replace them with ones that do. Pick ones that resonate with you and help you to feel powerful, bit like an affirmation. For me, it will be things like, "I always give my all – I can do anything, anything is possible." And, "Actually, money is made from paper that comes from trees, so money does grow on trees, and banks have branches!!" Or "I always seem to have enough money for everything I desire". This can really turn your life around.

As mentioned earlier, I see our beliefs as a web – similar to a spider's web or dreamcatcher. So what sort of web have you been building? Feeling rejected, unloved, a failure – these are not feelings – they are actually beliefs or perceptions. They are how you see yourself and what you are portraying to the world. They are what you will be building your web from and then catching, i.e. failure, rejection, non-love. Build a better web with what you really want to catch!

Release your FEARs and Trust

Another great exercise is to write out your fears, e.g. rejection, failure, feeling unsafe, being unloved, getting abandoned, and being alone. Once you have exposed them you can transform the fear. When you shine a light on fear it collapses. Have you heard the acronym for FEAR being "False Evidence Appearing Real"? That is what most of our fears are these days, not the old "we need to run because a lion is chasing us" fear. Our fears activate our adrenals, which can also cause ill-health and nervous anxiety, so we need to rein them in. There are lots of exercises we can do to calm our adrenals and hence anxiety.

Map of Consciousness
Developed By David R. Hawkins

	Name of Level	Energetic Log	Predominant Emotional State	View of Life	God-view	Process
Spiritual Paradigm	Enlightenment	700-1000	Ineffable	Is	Self	Pure Consciousness
	Peace	600	Bliss	Perfect	All-Being	Illumination
	Joy	540	Serenity	Complete	One	Transfiguration
	Love	500	Reverence	Benign	Loving	Revelation
Reason & Integrity	Reason	400	Understanding	Meaningful	Wise	Abstraction
	Acceptance	350	Forgiveness	Harmonious	Merciful	Transcendence
	Willingness	310	Optimism	Hopeful	Inspiring	Intention
	Neutrality	250	Trust	Satisfactory	Enabling	Release
	Courage	200	Affirmation	Feasible	Permitting	Empowerment
Survival Paradigm	Pride	175	Scorn	Demanding	Indifferent	Inflation
	Anger	150	Hate	Antagonistic	Vengeful	Aggression
	Desire	125	Craving	Disappointing	Denying	Enslavement
	Fear	100	Anxiety	Frightening	Punitive	Withdrawal
	Grief	75	Regret	Tragic	Disdainful	Despondency
	Apathy	50	Despair	Hopeless	Condemning	Abdication
	Guilt	30	Blame	Evil	Vindictive	Destruction
	Shame	20	Humiliation	Miserable	Despising	Elimination

In the map of consciousness, as shown again above, you will see that fear is back in the survival stage.

We cannot be in fear and love at the same time. You cannot feel jealousy or hatred and feel love. If you are able to vibrate in the energy of love, then people can't maintain their negative energy in that space, and so they will either drop their issue or leave. To get to this vibration, however, you need to ease yourself up the scale – it is not done overnight. You need to release your opinions of yourself and others to find the truth. If you can observe yourself and others without judgement, you will see the truth of who you both really are, beyond any previous conditioning and beliefs.

You can also list things you dislike – and where did those beliefs come from? Did you create them, or are they from a parent, teacher, or other influential person? Ask yourself what would happen if you had no resistance to your beliefs and perspectives and could just "observe them without judgement"? Rejection of situations often leads to chaos as your mind tries to control what is happening. Acceptance can often transform the situation.

Allow yourself to be vulnerable in these situations and when doing these exercises. Self-care and nourishment are really important. Trust that you can do this. There isn't a person I have met who hasn't experienced some form of trauma – yet our trauma always has a positive side – it is always unique to us and teaches us something that helps us cope in life. Can you find your blessings in the hurt, pain, and suffering? We are going to come to terms with our

past, accept it, and trust ourselves so that we can move forward.

Can You Face the Mirror?

Mirror work is fabulous – very confronting – but can make a difference as you start to see yourself in a different light. Look in the mirror and ask yourself, "What is the message I am giving out to the world?" How do you see yourself? Do you see a confident, happy, loving person, or do you say things to yourself such as, "I am fat, ugly, nervous, uncomfortable in my own skin, and no one could love me"? What are you saying to yourself?

I know this can be tricky and feel weird, but surrender to this process and be vulnerable, brave, raw! These thoughts about yourself are what you will be vibrating on an energetic level when you are in contact with other people. We want to realise what we are transmitting and transform this energy, so we can send out new messages and signals for others to pick up on. You can see this well in animals, especially dogs, as they are very sensitive, and they will often leave the room if someone is angry or comfort you if you feel down. They are picking up on your vibrations, your unique frequency. That is also why horses are used a lot to help with angry young teenagers. As the horses will not go near them while they are in a state, this teaches the kids to calm down.

Can you imagine looking in the mirror and feeling proud, feeling complete? It is possible you know! I hope you are beginning to feel that! Own yourself and be open to surprises! Be aware that as you step into your power, your mind may try to trick you and tell you things that aren't

true to pull you back to your old self where it feels "safe". It may give you thoughts such as, "You are a fraud, an imposter". Thank your mind, and tell it who you really are now. "I am strong, powerful, in charge." And be open to surprising yourself.

How Full Are You? Empty Your Subconscious

A great tool you can use to write out angry, sad, disempowering thoughts and beliefs is fast writing. Empty it all out, the good, the bad, and the ugly... When you think you are finished, keep going... Then destroy it, preferably burn it. If you are somewhere remote in nature, you can yell these things out – that feels amazing! It is great to reveal and clear out what is in your subconscious that you might not always be aware of. It is also wonderful to have a cold shower afterwards to clear out any remaining heavy energy. Another very conscious and energetically clearing exercise for emptying thoughts out is the 11x22s. I had some huge breakthroughs doing this exercise. I started with, "I am perfectly acceptable as I am" – boy, did some stuff come up then!

Revealing and Clearing the Subconscious 11x22s (The following is an excerpt from Mike Robinson, a man who inspired me greatly and helped me on my healing journey. (per listing in the references section)

"The subconscious is stored within our cells. To become truly aware of what is stored there, it is suggested that you do an 11x22 exercise. This is a very powerful technique, and many who have tried it have had miraculous results! There

are many powerful numbers which, when used as healing tools, can bring about dramatic changes. The process of using numbers with repeated positive sentences actually breaks down belief patterns. On an energetic level, the positive words enter into the mind and body, pushing out distorted energy. An internal shift then occurs as the distortion is dispersed through the aura, leaving it clear.

Positive Sentences

I have the right to be myself
I am perfectly acceptable as I am
I am in my power and I have abundant energy
I am well and healthy
I am fulfilling my life purpose and I have great joy and happiness
Money flows to me in a positive and abundant way right now
I am in a satisfying, fulfilling job, which I enjoy.

Sentences for Fear

I have the courage to achieve all that I desire
Life is perfect right now

Sentences for Anger

I am at peace with myself and the world
I express myself honestly in every moment

Sentence for Pride

I am equal to all life

Sentence for Illness

My.........(whichever part of the body is causing a problem) is perfect and clear.

Relationship Sentences

I have perfect relationships always
I am in a happy and fulfilling relationship

Choose one of the sentences and write it on a piece of paper. You then write down everything that comes into your mind, the positive, the negative, the silly, and the irrelevant. When you find a gap in the stream of thoughts that come into your mind, write the sentence you chose again, following it with the thoughts that rise in the mind. Keep this process of sentence, then thoughts, sentence, then thoughts, etc., until you have done the sentence followed by the thoughts twenty-two times. You then do the same every day for eleven days.

If at any time you write the sentence and nothing comes into your mind, then repeat the sentence to yourself. If the mind is still blank, write the words, 'no thoughts and no feelings', then carry on writing the sentence. It is possible that this may appear eight or nine times, then suddenly thoughts come back into the mind. You know when you are on top of a blockage when the mind becomes completely blank.

It does not matter if your thoughts are extremely negative or if swear words appear. This energy has to come out and be expressed on paper. The 11x22s are better when they are handwritten, but as long as all your thoughts come out, typewritten or done on a computer is acceptable. You will notice the stream of thoughts from the subconscious, things you are not consciously aware of and whose context may surprise you.

Whilst you are writing the 11x22s, make sure you are not disturbed, so turn off the telephone and lock the door. It is also important to do the 22 sentences all in one sitting, so you may need half an hour to two hours each day, maybe even longer when you first start the process. See it as time to set aside for your healing, for your growth.

If you choose to make up your own sentence, it must only contain positive words. For example, 'I have no fear' would not work because the word 'fear' will attract the energy of fear towards it. The idea is to remove the negative thoughts from the mind. You may find, whilst writing, you seem to go into what is currently called 'channelling' where a lot of information seems to come through, or your thoughts seem to be using the term 'you' instead of 'I'. Whatever is happening, keep writing it down. If you have found a lot of issues have surfaced at the end of the day, then you can burn the papers, or you can wait until the end of the eleven days and burn them all together. It is important that at the end of the eleven-day process you rest for eleven days before starting another sentence. If you start the process but forget to do a day, then you need to start again from day one. This is because the blocked energy is moving through the energy bodies. If you stop before it is released, it begins to slide back to its original state.

I have used this technique over the last seven years. When I first tried it, I used the sentence, 'I am well and healthy.' I had been suffering from an ache in the lower part of my stomach, and on day eight, I suddenly got a flashback of someone trying to abuse me when I was a child. I saw myself running and hiding in a cupboard, which I locked from the inside. At the same time as the flashback, I felt the

ache move up through my body and disappear through my mind and be released. This proved to me that we store memories within the body because after that the ache was gone. This is a very powerful healing technique, but it does demand action when anything is revealed to you. After seeing this episode of being chased, I carried on with the next sentence. I then saw an image that appeared to be a past life memory of myself in Egypt chasing the man who chased me. In that moment there was an instant act of acceptance, forgiveness, and love. The karma had been played out.

7x72s

If you find the eleven-day process too long, you can use exactly the same principle, but instead of writing the sentence followed by the thoughts twenty-two times, you write it seventy-two times over seven days. The effect is still the same, but you may find you will need more time each day to accomplish the task.

3x75s

When you have completed the 11x22s on a few occasions, you can use the 3x75s. This is less powerful than the 11x22s and 7x72s but quicker and still dynamic. First choose a positive sentence, and then write down this sentence seventy-five times one after the other in succession. There is no need to follow the sentence with any thoughts. At the end, enter into your feelings and allow any emotions to surface. If you feel the need to write down your thoughts and feelings then do so. Repeat this process for the following two days. You must then leave a gap of three days before starting another one."

We are like a glass full of milk. While we hold all these old disempowering thoughts and beliefs, there is no room for the new to come in, and your milk will become curdled. Clearing some of these limiting ideas is like emptying the glass and washing it out. It allows room for new beliefs and experiences to come in – you can fill your glass with liquid gold. This too is gold – realising that your opinions are not set in stone and that you can let go of a lot of stubbornness that most often doesn't serve you. You can then start telling yourself a different, better-feeling story about you and all the things that are important to you. Make it uplifting and magical, and feel how that transforms your energy and your feelings. Remember the spider's web or dreamcatcher – think about what you would really like to build and create for your life. Stop any little voice that tries to figure out how or says it isn't possible.

Do you remember when you first began to dream of all that life could be? Remember what it felt like to be truly excited and not have this dead, empty feeling inside? Can you remember jumping out of bed in the morning, eager to start the day and excited to see what was going to happen? Let's start moving towards your dreams again rather than away from them. Let's begin to feel really excited to begin your day.

If you find these ideas difficult or confronting, will you allow someone else to help you learn how to find and change your beliefs and create a life you'll love? For years I tried to do everything myself, not wanting to bother others or thinking I was not worth it and they wouldn't understand or even be able to help me. I especially didn't want anyone to really see the real me – not that I even knew who she was!

Reaching out for help and guidance and having mentors who could cheer me on and help remind me has made a huge difference.

Follow-Up Exercises – Avoidance and Completion

If you haven't completed the questions and exercises from above, then I have included them below, so you can do them now. I know I would avoid questions and exercises as they would feel too confronting; however, my biggest breakthroughs came through actually doing what was suggested. So please give them a go for your own sake. Especially the 11x22s – you will not regret it as they are SOOOO freeing!

Once again, if you feel your trauma is too great, then do not do these on your own, and please seek some assistance.

- List some of your beliefs and judgements that you are aware of in your life, and also those that you see in the world around you. Consciously choose to keep or transform each belief, and see if there are beliefs in the world around you that help you transform your existing beliefs into more empowering ones. (As you observe your beliefs and judgements, you will be astounded to see what else comes up that you were totally unaware of).

- What is the story that runs in you when you are pushed? For example, one story could be, "I am no good, no one loves me". Can you ask yourself, "Why do I have that belief or hold that perspective? Where

did it come from?"

- Starting with your parents or your main caregiver(s) from childhood, and any other influential people in your life, ask yourself, "What did they believe about me and who I should be? What did they think I should look like and do with my life? And what were their beliefs and ideas about marriage, career, children, money, and religion?

- What sort of spider's web have you been unconsciously weaving with your beliefs? What might be the kind of web you would really like to build? What is it that you would like to attract?

- Write out the things you are fearful of, any fears of rejection, failure, feeling unsafe, being unloved, getting hurt, feeling abandoned or being alone. It might even be things you didn't think you were afraid of, for example, success or being loved.

- You can also list things you dislike. Where did those beliefs come from? Did you create them, or are they from a parent, teacher, or other influential person? Ask yourself what would happen if you had no resistance to your beliefs and perspectives and could just "observe them without judgement"?

- Can you find the blessings in any hurt, pain, and suffering you may have experienced?

- Look in the mirror, and ask yourself, "What is the message I am giving out to the world? How do I see

myself? Do I see a confident, happy, loving person? What am I saying to myself? Is it things such as "I am fat, ugly, nervous, and uncomfortable in my own skin, and no one will love me"?

- Can you start to nourish those parts that have been unnourished and give them some love? Can you acknowledge what you might admire and begin to feel a little bit grateful for some of your traits? Even if you start by saying, "Well, my eyes are a pretty colour", or "I am grateful I have a heart that pumps my blood and nourishes my body." I am sure you get the gist of what I am talking about.

- What dreams do you have or have you had as a child? How could your life look?

"If reality can destroy dreams then dreams can destroy reality"

—*Conway Stone*

Once you become aware of some of your limiting beliefs, you can then begin to bring in more powerful self-talk with affirmations. Here are some that have helped me.

A Few Useful Affirmations to Start With

I WANT TO BE WELL
I AM HAPPY AND CONTENT
I ALWAYS HAVE A CHOICE
I AM WORTHY
I NOW TAKE MY POWER BACK
I AM SUCCESSFUL
I CREATE MY LIFE

MY LIFE IS WORTH LIVING
I AM LUCKY
I AM NEEDED
I AM FULL OF ENERGY
I FEEL VIBRANT
I AM HEALTHY
I SLEEP LIKE A BABY
I FEEL CALM AND RELAXED
I ONLY FEEL LIKE EATING HEALTHY FOOD
MY BODY IS AMAZING
MY EYESIGHT IS AMAZING
I LOVE TO EXERCISE
I RELEASE ALL THE CONTROL MY FAMILY HAS OVER ME
I SPEND TIME NURTURING MYSELF, WHICH GIVES ME THE ENERGY TO GIVE TO OTHERS
I ENJOY THE TIME I GIVE TO ME
I SEE AND APPRECIATE THE SUCCESSES IN MY DAILY LIFE
I AM PRODUCTIVE

Chapter 6

Forgiveness of Self and Others to Find Gratitude and Peace

"It's one of the greatest gifts you can give yourself, to forgive. Forgive everybody."

—Maya Angelou

Every Experience Has a Gift

I know everywhere talks about forgiveness and gratitude, and these two things can be really difficult. While forgiveness of others wasn't so hard, it took me a really long time to forgive myself and to feel true gratitude for life. However, once you get it you will see that EVERY experience has a gift, and you can be at peace with whatever happens, knowing that not only did you create that experience so you could learn, but in learning the lesson, you are also about to go to a whole new level!

By forgiving we can release and transform guilt and fear, such as the fear of rejection, fear of love, fear of criticism, fear of not being good enough, or fear of punishment. We can realise we don't need to be perfect or understand everything – it is ok to be vulnerable. We can respond rather than react, enabling our heart and energy to expand. We

can absolve ourselves from any vicious, unconscious cycles of anger and guilt that we might be caught in.

I'd like to share with you one of my proven successful techniques for forgiving others. One of the best things about this simple technique is that it's step-by-step. Once you get the hang of it, the best people to focus on forgiving are those who you are closest with or those who were most influential in your life. Just go with what comes up for you first. If you have extremely harsh and traumatic experiences, remember, please don't do this on your own but seek some help and guidance and someone to support you.

How To Truly Forgive Others and Set Yourself Free

Here's a simplified variation of one of the Forgiveness Exercises I have learned for experiences. Just start on something simple that you might be angry about for now.

Step 1: Set the Scene

Close your eyes and for a couple of minutes, bring back all the anger, frustration, and pain you felt when you believed someone in your life had wronged you. Feel yourself in the moment of when it happened, picturing the same environment you were in when you interacted with them.

Step 2: Feel the Anger and Pain

As you see the person(s) who "wronged" you in front of you, get emotional. Relive the anger and pain. Feel it burn. Don't resist the feelings – let them come up and out, and

observe the feelings without judging them. This should not take long (if it is too long, you are getting caught in it), it should just be like you are watching a movie on a screen or listening to a recording – you can experience the feelings but don't judge them.

Once you bring up the emotions that these people created in you, move onto the next step...

Step 3: Forgive Into Love

See that same person(s) in front of you, but instead, feel compassion for them, realising that they have merely been reflecting something to you that you believed about yourself – that you were somehow a bad person, unworthy, unloveable, or undeserving.

Step 4: Ask yourself:

What did I believe about myself that caused this to occur?
What did I learn from this?
How did this situation make my life better?

It helps me to think of a quote from Neale Donald Walsch, "[God] sent you nothing but angels." Or I think of, "Forgive them Father for they know not what they do".

To give you a simple example: When I was working through things, I imagined a time at school when I had been bullied by some girls in my class, and one girl in particular, who I thought was my friend. I imagined the playground we were in at the time and remembered the pain of them not wanting to play with me, and saying I was boring and telling me to go away.

When I went back into my experience, I believed at the time that I was boring, didn't know enough, and wasn't funny or pretty enough to be in the group. So this is what I got from the girls – rejection – because I was rejecting myself. It has made my life better because I have now learnt that they were merely mirrors of how I felt about myself. My soul was asking me to look at that aspect of what I was doing to myself (which I didn't realise at the time).

I then spent a lot of my life trying to be "fun and popular", so I could fit in rather than being me, and I was still often ignored or rejected. Now that I have learnt that I can just be me and feel worthy about myself, I am no longer rejected but welcomed!

A friend actually ran into the ringleader of this group who had bullied me not long after I did this exercise. Let's call the ringleader Robyn. Well Robyn asked my friend to send me her apologies and ask for my forgiveness, as she had always felt so bad about how she treated me back in school. She had also been going through a hard time and had been trying to hide it. Robyn said she didn't know why she was so nasty, she just couldn't seem to help herself and never forgave herself. I was so miserable at the time that my parents took me out of the school. I had no idea that she would even remember me. I guess this shows that it was really me in victim mode causing her to act out. For every victim there is always a bully and vice versa – as they say, it takes 2 to tango!

Others are Mirrors Reflecting Our Insecurities and Doubts

Everyone who has ever entered our lives, even those who have hurt us, are nothing more than someone in front of us teaching us an important lesson. They are mirrors of what is going on within us (I never felt good enough, worthy enough, so I attracted people to make sure I felt that way fully). Focus on the fact that you deserve love, and put this feeling into your subconscious. Let go of your struggle, and change your feelings by forgiving yourself so that you can heal your reactive patterns and express exactly who you are with truth and love. What you are really upset about is deep in your subconscious. Ask yourself, "What am I REALLY upset about?" You will find it is always the same feeling, and it comes from the same root. Your mind is what gets hurt when you get upset and hold grudges. You think you are powerless, you are not!

Think about what lessons you could derive from your situations, as painful as they might be. And believe me, I do understand that for some people these lessons are incredibly painful. How did these lessons make you better? Or help you grow? What can you now let go of? If this is too painful or traumatic for you, I advise working with a professional.

Compassion for Others

Next, think about who this person is or was at the time. What pain or anguish could they have gone through in their lives that made them do what they did? You will often find that people who hurt others are crying out themselves. There

is a saying, "Hurt people hurt people" because it is true. This implies that those who hurt others are usually doing it because at some level they were hurt too. So think about how they may have been hurt in their own childhood or in their recent years, or what they were really trying to show you about themselves or yourself. What this does is extinguishes the pain of what happened, so it no longer eats at you.

You don't have to ask the other person to forgive you. You just have to forgive them. That's completely within your control and takes you away from being a victim. Be aware that if you are holding onto anger or hatred, that continues to live in your energy field and will stop love from coming into your field. Also, feeling hateful or vengeful towards someone may hurt them energetically, but it is way more harmful to you, so let it go.

To truly forgive someone means there is no resistance or negative energy to your thoughts about them. Have you seen the movie with Jim Carrey, "The Truman Show"? I believe this is what's really going on. We are living in a movie, and you are the star; the other people are just actors in the movie, there to press your buttons and make the movie a bit more exciting. To escape from the movie, you need to have no reaction to those buttons. If you can see others as merely actors wanting you to react, you're able to get on with your life without having to waste your energy on them. When you no longer react, you might find what you perceive as negative people don't even enter your space anymore. When you choose love, you become the change you wish to see in the world around you, and your world changes.

I find it is helpful to remember that we all have every emotion within us, and we all make mistakes. Rather than being righteous about how we have been wronged, it is helpful to look within and see where we might do or have done something similar. I was angry at Robyn for shutting me out of the group; however, there have been times when in my trying to be popular, I too have been cruel to others in some way and shut them out. I have also exhibited the same behaviour in the past by being cruel to my mother in many ways and shutting her out. It's good to notice these things and forgive all involved.

Reframing Your Experiences

A great exercise to do if you have had a falling out with someone or lost your cool with them is: When you go to bed at night, review any challenging events during the day. You can ask yourself, If I was coming from my Higher Self, then…

1. How would I have acted differently?
2. What would I have said?
3. In what way could I have made the situation better?
4. What have I learnt from this experience?
5. What is the blessing?

You can then replay the situation from this higher perspective in a way the other person could receive it. This will remain in your subconscious, so next time you are more likely to respond and act differently too.

Learning to Forgive Yourself

Once you have forgiven others, the most important person to forgive is yourself. Write yourself a long letter (or in my case book lol!) in your journal, apologising for all the harsh and harmful things you have said and done to yourself, all the thoughts, words, actions, and feelings – keep writing till you feel empty, and undoubtedly will have had a good cry. It is important to be the observer, the witness of this. Preferably go out and do it in nature and make sure you have privacy and can be undisturbed. It can be overwhelming to see what you have been thinking, so please focus on doing this without judging yourself even more. Once you have got it all out, then write to yourself saying how you would like to be treated, what words and actions make you feel better and feel loved.

You might have come to realise that even though others have done some terrible and perhaps what you once might have perceived as unforgivable things, no one has been worse to you than yourself. It has also been your judgement and an ongoing replay in your head of situations, relationships, and experiences that have kept you stuck in the negative emotions of hate, anger, guilt, blame, shame, etc.

Finding Gratitude Will Change Your Attitude

Once you have forgiven yourself and others, it is much easier to feel gratitude. Once you do start to feel gratitude, your life really starts to open up.

Sometimes when we are starting out it can be hard to truly feel gratitude if life is just being really shitty! I know I struggled with this for a while, and gratitude seemed elusive. However, if we look closely, we discover that life delivers us many hidden gifts. If you focus on looking for the hidden treasures or sparkles of light, you may find the smallest of things can allow your heart and soul to blossom and glow. Go outside and look for something beautiful in nature, or if you are not able to find any nature, focus on the fact that you can breathe. And if you breathe deeply, as we have discussed previously, you will find you just feel a whole lot better. Gratitude is also wonderful at bringing you into mindfulness and quieting your mind. As per the map of consciousness, you can't feel grateful and angry or grateful and despondent at the same time.

You can also start with basic gratitudes for the day, feeling grateful for your home, the food you have to eat, the water you have to drink, and the fact that you have shelter or even bedding. There might be a life lesson you are truly grateful for right now, such as something you have learnt, a special relationship with someone, or a skill you have. You might be grateful for a person, being, or animal that is present in your life in this moment (may even just be the thought of them). Perhaps you can even feel the love and support they have for you.

Have a go at saying to yourself for 30 days, "Every day I'm feeling better and better". As you do improve each day, you can also feel the gratitude of this taking effect. If you say this to yourself with conviction, each day will be better, and you will feel gratitude for what YOU have created in your life. You will also be a lot more in the present moment

and will notice all the things that are better in your life. Have you ever noticed that if you start thinking about, say, a red car, then you start seeing them everywhere? This is the same principle – it is the law of attraction.

When you are living in depression, it is impossible to be grateful, as you are telling yourself there is nothing to be grateful for. This is what you continue to get – this is your web of attraction – "I am ungrateful" – because you have pushed anything that might help you feel grateful away. I found this was another belief that I had to delete, "I am ungrateful," as it was something often said to me as a child. "You ungrateful child," or "You selfish girl," and "You don't deserve anything". Not to disparage the people who said it, as they really didn't know any better and were doing the best they knew how at the time. Generally, it was what was said to them as a child. So once you delete beliefs like this – things that were said to you – it can make an amazing difference to your life. While I think of it, another beauty I had to delete was, "Children should be seen and not heard", which made it very hard for me to speak up later in life. I am grateful I have now deleted these beliefs and installed more empowering ones!

Awareness and forgiveness without a different action are useless. When you truly forgive yourself and others, you will act, think, feel, and speak differently. Words create our world, so speak and write whatever it is you want (with the feeling that it is already done, by having gratitude for it.) To watch your thinking, you need to breathe slowly and consciously with presence, observe without judgement, and listen without thinking. Action is the law of cause and effect. Thought is the cause, and reality is the physical effect

that shows in our world. If you think and feel differently, you will act differently, and you will feel gratitude. So line up your thoughts and feelings with what it is you really want to experience.

There are plenty of studies showing that people who are grateful receive more to be grateful for! Gratitude will change your attitude! Your attitude in how you approach life and the effort you put into maintaining this is more important than your past, your finances, your current circumstances, your education, your success, or what others think, say, or do. It can make all the difference in your life. Every day we are given a choice as to how we will embrace our lives, how we will show up, who we will be. I now know that life is absolutely 10% of what happens to us and 90% how we react and respond. We are the ones with all the power, so embrace your life every day. Even if it is difficult now, start giving it a go and watch the transformation of your life slowly come into play – it may even be speedy!

I promise you will be absolutely astounded at what happens when you have an attitude of gratitude. When you are in gratitude you will be more in your heart, loving, and at peace. There is no room for depression in that space. This is the gold, you are transformed as your heart and energy expand.

Follow-Up exercises – Get in Touch With You, Forgive and Release

Once again, if you haven't completed the questions and exercises from above, then please do them now. These

exercises will really help you to empty out even further and truly get in touch with your soul. Please seek help if they trigger any overwhelming feelings.

- Make a list of all the people you feel have wronged you or all the things you are angry about, and use the forgiveness exercise with them.

  Step 1: Set the Scene
  Step 2: Feel the Anger and Pain
  Step 3: Forgive Into Love

  Now Ask yourself:
  What did I believe about myself that caused this to occur?
  What did I learn from this?
  How did this situation make my life better?

- If something is or was deeply upsetting, ask yourself, "What am I REALLY upset about?" When you get to an answer then ask what is really behind that answer and continue asking yourself questions until you find out what is really going on at the root of the issue. You will then come to realise what has been bringing you the experiences and feelings you have had throughout your life. (For example, my thinking no one ever listens is me being upset about not feeling they are acknowledging me, which stems from the fact that I felt my parents didn't acknowledge me and in fact deep down I was not acknowledging myself and everyone else is just a mirror.)

- What are the hidden lessons you can extract from some of your painful experiences? How did these lessons make you better or help you grow? After digesting the lessons, what can you now let go of?

- Thinking about the person(s) who has wronged you and who they were at the time, consider what pain or anguish they could have gone through in their lives that made them do what they did. Can you forgive them for probably not knowing any better or for coming from a place of hurt or unconsciousness themselves?

- Try reframing your not-so-good experiences at the end of the day by asking yourself, "If I was coming from my Higher Self, then…"

How would I have acted differently?
What would I have said?
In what way could I have made the situation better?
What have I learnt from this experience?
What is the blessing?

Then replay the situation.

- If possible go into nature or find a quiet spot, and write yourself a long letter or in your journal apologising for all the harsh and harmful things you have said and done to yourself, all the thoughts, words, actions and feelings. Be mindful to be the witness of this only and not go into judgement. Keep writing till you feel empty.

- Write out what you feel grateful for and continue doing this, as well as thinking about it during the day.

- Commit to waking each day with a positive affirmation, for example, "Every day is getting better and better", or "I am going to have an incredible day today", or ask, "How can my day be incredible today?" Continue to be on the lookout to see what appears, occurs and if necessary act on that if you feel moved to.

- Become conscious of what you are thinking, feeling, saying, and doing as much as possible. Observe this in yourself, and bring conscious awareness to the thoughts, feelings, words, and actions without judgement, so you can transform.

"There are so many things in the world that could be invisible to the material eye, and when you take a moment to stop, to pause, to be present and notice them—that's gratitude."

—Jay Shetty

Chapter 7

Reconnecting – Finding Freedom and Love

"Love starts when we push aside our ego and make room for someone else."

—*Rudolf Steiner*

We really need to reconnect with who we are and raise our vibration (if needed refer to the map of consciousness), to feel freedom and love. To let go of this old shell, the old you you thought you were. We have done the work to transform a lot of our old feelings, which will now enable you to really start seeing who you are and feeling worthy of love. When we reconnect, we realise we no longer need to control ourselves and others. You realise you are energy and are always looked after.

Can you allow yourself to just be yourself? Love yourself for who you are, not what others want you to be or how you think they want you to be. This will enable us to come from our heart and be authentic, and others will see this. It will allow us to embrace our emotions without constantly judging them. To accept all aspects of ourselves, including emotions that sometimes happen in life – we are all going

to experience disappointment, frustration, pain, sorrow, grief, guilt, etc.; however, now we can look at it differently and allow it to pass.

I think the analogy of the orange being squeezed is awesome. So when you squeeze an orange, what comes out is what is inside – in the orange's case it is sweet juice – well unless it is off, then it is bitter and yucky! So it is with us when we are pressured. If you explode or cry when you are under pressure, then there is work to be done; it is like you have been left in the sun and turned sour. You can change your life by realising what's inside and healing any bitter, sour, or off parts, so you can become your true self and free yourself of the internal struggles.

Responding Instead of Reacting

I still get triggered; however, now I have tools and ways of being that I have embedded. One of the best tools is to get into nature, get my feet on the ground, just breathe, and ask myself, "What are my thoughts and feelings about this? What could my message be, and what action do I need to take?" Sometimes you do need to take action, but remember it is about responding, not reacting. Sometimes it is best to remove yourself from the situation. No one is perfect. We all slip up at times. If you do, it is about getting back on the horse and giving it another go.

Perhaps you might realise you need some more help with whatever the issue is, so seek that. I found that one kinesiology or healing session, such as Energy Reset was equivalent to about ten visits to the psychiatrist or psychologist.

Animals are a wonderful way to get in touch and feel unconditional love. I love how they are always so in tune with how you are feeling and just want to love you and for you to love them – or play with them and pat them. We all need nourishment and love.

Even though you might not feel it to start with, just remember there is no separation from your true self or others. We are all connected. I love to connect with my inner being each morning. To say, "Show me how powerful I am. What miracle and magic can I create today? Today is going to be awesome!" This is an amazing thing to say to yourself. Your Higher Self loves you to ask questions and loves to connect with you.

Play With Life

As I have mentioned previously, the words you use with yourself and the emotion you put into them can totally change your perspective, your actions, and how life and others treat you. It is awesome to begin to play with life – to constantly ask to be shown things. If I lose something, I ask for help to find it. I love to play games such as "Please show me a feather today", and I will undoubtedly see one if I am looking. This cements in for you that the Universe and your Higher Self (however you like to think of it) are listening.

I also notice that I will get a lot of messages in songs, books, or things coming into my email or on social media, which are exactly what I have been asking for or what I need to hear, learn, or see at that point in time. The spirit world loves to connect with us in this way – even number

plates can hold a message. Symbols are a great way we can receive messages.

You can tune into your body and see if you can think, feel, or see a symbol that is trying to convey something to you. You might see a chain around your throat if you are having trouble speaking. You can then remove this chain and transform the energy of it by either sending it to the Earth to be transformed into compost (and that compost can then grow a lush garden), you can place it in an imagined fire, or you can send it to the ether to be transformed into butterflies or light. I have oracle cards which seem to always give me the perfect wisdom or message I need in that moment. There are so many ways we can connect if we start asking and noticing.

Embodying Your I AM

I spoke in an earlier chapter about your "I AM" – this is a very strengthening affirmation for your body – you are talking to your soul, your inner being. It also gives you a boundary and connects you to your body if you do it with movement – I put my hands on my heart and say, "I AM the I AM", and then take one arm to the sky and one to the ground to ground my place with heaven, the Universe, all that is and my place here on Earth, and I affirm "This is ME".

I do this every morning and imagine the inner spark of life within my chest (around the thymus) exploding into light and strengthening my sense of self. To me this means I am love, I am the creator of my own life, I am balanced, I am God within, and everything is up to me. I say this three times with conviction and ground myself strongly afterwards. I am not sure how you feel about God or

the Universe – it is about finding something higher than yourself that is meaningful to you that you can connect with. So substitute my words with whatever you believe in. What is your I AM? This is how you can send your message to yourself, the Universe, and the world. When you say your I AM, you will feel your power, take it back, and begin to change yourself and the world around you. This is your choice to take back your life. Your I AM can be whatever you make it. I AM Powerful, I AM Loved, I AM a great mother. I AM the creator of my own destiny. I AM who I choose to become. So have a play with this, and create an empowering I AM for yourself.

Remembering and Reconnecting – What is Your Soul's Message?

If your energy is feeling scattered, remembering your soul's message can help you to ground, integrate, and become whole. It is about remembering who we are and why we came here and becoming that. It is time to seize the day and focus on the truth of who you are and realise you are LOVE. That is really all there is. It is at this stage that you might also start to remember it is not all about you all the time – our self-indulgence takes a bit of a back seat. We have needed to learn to love ourselves fully and connect within to enable us to send genuine love out to all. However, just as we are here for ourselves, we are here to support and love others as well and to make our special mark in the world.

What service can you give to the world? What is your soul's message? What is your reason for coming here at this point in time? Your service might be to raise an incredible

human being or to hold a loving space for others, or it might be to invent or create something that is going to totally change the world. If you are unsure, you might be able to find someone to help guide you or just sit with things and journal for a while. I am quite certain everyone has a special gift. I believe we are love. And I believe that in solving your suffering, you will have helped all of humanity.

What is Freedom?

Freedom is about being unshakeable in your power, being able to connect within. And if you don't know how to respond to something, freedom is about surrendering into not knowing and asking within for what you need. Freedom is becoming conscious. How can you align with the forces that conspire with us to grow and evolve? Can you release the busy-ness of the mind and go into the moment and allow the flow of love and wisdom from your heart and soul. To become strong within, you constantly need to watch, check, and let go of your thoughts, feelings, words, and actions and live in the present. Today is a gift, that is why they call it the present, so appreciate that you have this moment. It will never come again. If I am feeling shaky or out of alignment for some reason and can't get myself in order, I seek help from my mentors or other therapists. It is ok to ask for help.

Ho'oponopono Prayer

Another great tool I often use for connecting is Ho'oponopono. This is a traditional Hawaiian prayer about putting things right, about responsibility, love, forgiveness, and personal power. Translated into English, the word means "correction". I find it very powerful to say to myself

as it seems to speak to my soul. I find this works really well for me, especially when I first started using it.

The Ho'oponopono Prayer

Thank You
I Love You
Please Forgive Me
I'm Sorry

The basis of the prayer is that there is no such thing as "out there" – everything happens to you in your mind. Everything you see, everything you hear, every person you meet, you experience in your mind. You only think it's "out there", and you think that absolves you of responsibility. In fact it's quite the opposite: you are responsible for everything you think and everything that comes to your attention. It sounds harsh, but it means that if you create everything in your life, you are also able to clear it, clean it, and, through forgiveness, change it.

Gratitude – THANK YOU

Say "THANK YOU" – it doesn't really matter who or what you're thanking. Thank your body for all it does for you. Thank yourself for being the best you can be. Thank God. Thank the Universe or whoever resonates with you.

Love – I LOVE YOU

Say I LOVE YOU. Say it to your body, say it to God, the Universe, or your Higher Self. Say I LOVE YOU to yourself, to your nearest and dearest and your enemies, to the air you

breathe, to the home that shelters you. Say I LOVE YOU to your challenges. Say it over and over. Mean it. Feel it. There is nothing as powerful as Love.

Ask Forgiveness – PLEASE FORGIVE ME

Don't worry about who you're asking. Just ask! PLEASE FORGIVE ME. Say it over and over. Put as much meaning as you can into it!

Repentance – I'M SORRY

You are responsible for everything in your mind, even if it seems to be "out there." Once you realise that, it's very natural to feel sorry. This realisation that we create everything can be painful, and you will likely resist accepting responsibility for the "out there" kind of problems until you start to practice this method on your more obvious "in here" problems and see results.

So choose something that you already know you've caused for yourself, such as depression, weight or health issues, addictions, anger, or relationship issues. Think of the issue and say I'M SORRY. What you are really saying is, "I realise that I am responsible for this (issue) in my life, and I feel terribly sorry that something in my consciousness has caused this. I am sorry that I haven't connected more with you or listened to you more, my inner being, my Higher Self."

Become Aware, Be Courageous, Wise and Discerning

Once we reconnect with our true-self we can really be courageous, even outrageous! We realise we do have free

will, and this will, used wisely, can change our lives for the better. We can allow ourself to be confronted so that we can be our best self. Through what we see as our limitations or challenges, we can ask ourselves what we are denying or restricting in ourselves. By watching where we might self-sabotage and by asking great questions, we can break through these limitations. We then land in the flow. Life does not have to be a struggle as we once believed. It is not all about hard work; it is about connecting and getting into the flow – to me this is freedom. We escape the control of our mind and our old ways of thinking.

Rather than just accepting everything that is going on around you, ask yourself how discerning you are. What questions are you asking about what is going on in the world? Contemplate some of the things we hear and take for granted from the media and government, and make your own decisions.

Awareness is the key to mastering your life. You have everything you need to shift out of any negative focus and into a higher frequency the moment you become aware of what you are doing and saying, who you are being, and what you are thinking. Through this, you can become aware of who you are. You will discover that you have a soul and what your soul is calling you to do. You will remember why you're here and what your life is about – it is about reconnecting with your soul and learning its agenda for your life. You will then be able to stand in your own life and light and feel absolute freedom. You will realise you do deserve all that life has to offer, and you will feel true compassion and love for yourself. You will feel free of those old shackles of depression. You will feel transformed into gold!

Follow-Up exercises – Talk to Your Soul

Answer the following questions in your journal, and practise the exercises to really communicate with your inner being.

- Can you allow yourself to just be yourself? Love yourself for who you are, not what others want you to be or how you think they want you to be.

- Who are you really?

- Who are you becoming or remembering yourself to be?

- Is there anything else you need to release?

- Find a tool or way of being to help you if you get triggered. One of the best tools I use is to get into nature, get my feet on the ground, just breathe, and ask myself, "What are my thoughts and feelings about this? What could my message be, and what action do I need to take?"

- If it resonates, when triggered, you can practise *The Ho'oponopono Prayer*

Thank You
I Love You
Please Forgive Me
I'm Sorry

You can easily say this in your head whenever your emotions get the better of you. I find it very calming.

- Connect with your inner being each morning. Say, "Show me how powerful I am. What miracle and magic can I create today? Today is going to be awesome!"

- Talk to your Higher Self during the day, and ask questions to connect with your inner being.

- Begin to play with life – constantly ask to be shown things. This is really helpful if you can't find something. Simply ask, "Where might those keys be?" Then let it go, and they will turn up effortlessly.

- Can you notice any messages in songs, books, cars, signs, or things coming into your email or on social media which are exactly what you have been asking for or what you need to hear, see, or learn at this point in time? Even the fact that Facebook hears everything you say and sends you adverts of exactly what you are talking about can be handy!

- Tune into your body, and see if you can think, feel, or see a symbol that is trying to convey something to you. Perhaps messages may also come in dreams.

- Ensure you are grounding yourself every morning and tuning into yourself rather than rushing off without grounding, even if it is just a couple of minutes in the shower.

- What is your I AM? Your I AM can be whatever you make it, for example, I AM Powerful, I AM Loved, I AM a

great mother. I AM the creator of my own destiny. I AM who I choose to become. Have a play with this, and create an empowering I AM for yourself.

- What service can you give to the world? What is your soul's message? What is your reason for coming here at this point in time? What can I do next to make a difference to myself, my family and my community?

- How FREE are you becoming? To become wise, strong, and free within yourself, constantly watch, check, and let go of your thoughts, feelings, words, and actions. And live in the present.

- Rather than just accepting everything that is going on around you, ask yourself, "How discerning am I? What questions am I asking about what is going on in the world?" Contemplate some of the things you hear and take for granted from the media and government, and make your own decisions.

- Use the key of awareness to master your life. Ask yourself, "What do I have within me right now to shift out of any negative focus and into a higher frequency in this moment? What better-feeling thing can I do, say, think, and be in this moment to align with my Higher Self?" What is one step that will help me move forward?

"Nothing is more important than reconnecting with your bliss. Nothing is as rich. Nothing is more real."
—Deepak Chopra

My Prayer

We stand in Light
We stand united
Through Love we are invincible.

May Divine Order be restored on earth.
May Justice reign supreme,
A mighty Flame of Light.
May my will, my loving Heart
Touch all, free all, release all.

Tongues of Holy Fire
Ignite obstacles to Love
Tongues of Holy Fire
Transform and transfigure.
Tongues of Holy Fire
Descending unto Earth.

From my loving Heart
Let light descend.
From my loving Heart
A rain of blessings fall.
Doves fly free.
The Mothers work through Me.

— Chandra Easton
http://www.starastrologyhealing.com/

Transformation –
Let the Magic Begin!

"Bravery and adventure! That's the ticket! Don't sit and gather moss. Get up, get out, do what you dream of doing, and if it doesn't work, it doesn't work, and you don't need to make that particular mistake again, but at least you won't get old wondering what if you had."

— Garrison Keillor

Soul Integration – To Become the Butterfly

Welcome to a whole new world – this is where you can truly become the beautiful butterfly – light and free. The precious diamond that was formed under such immense pressure. The transformation of depression into gold and finding your inner spark and your own brilliance is now within your reach. Expansion, exhilaration, courage, compassion, confidence, empowerment, appreciation, radiance, brilliance, love, joy, gratitude, and deep peace are all who you can become should you so choose. Be like Neo in The Matrix and take the red pill (representing truth

and power), and come down the rabbit hole to discover yourself. Find your inner wizard, and realise all you can be. Take ownership of yourself, your free will, and your power. Link your mind, heart, and soul to become the embodiment of your true, authentic self.

When you start loving and appreciating yourself and giving more than taking, you begin to catapult yourself to a whole new level, and the possibilities seem endless. You begin attracting all sorts of people and heartfelt, loving feelings and experiences you could never have imagined in your wildest dreams. Or perhaps you did imagine them, and that is why they then show up in your reality!

Is Your Soul Screaming at You?

It took me many years to write this book; I was always too busy, and it seemed there were many other things needing to be done. It has been in my consciousness a long time. Something that really inspired me to share what I have learnt with you was an esoteric astrology reading that I had. I found this incredible as it was a reading of my stars showing where I have been and where my soul is at. My soul was screaming at me to get on with things. It was as if I had drawn out a library full of books but was not sharing or imparting the wisdom and knowledge I had gained and was hoarding all the books in the closet! Ha! This was when I became aware that it isn't just about me. We all have a calling, an obligation to become our best selves, so we can assist others to become their best selves and shift consciousness throughout the world.

Recently, I was lucky enough to take a trip with my husband to Uluru. We had both felt so drawn to the energy of the

Rock in the centre of Australia, which was incredible. It is known as the Earth's solar plexus chakra. The solar plexus chakra, amongst other things, has to do with wisdom and processing emotion. Uluru acts as a type of umbilical cord to the planet and maintains life all around the globe.

Being at Uluru and Kata Tjuta opened my eyes to the enormity and presence of energy all around us and to the sacredness of our own presence once we still our mind. You could feel the ancientness and wisdom in the very core of your being. The deep knowing from thousands of years. I hope you can feel the calling too, for you to become present, to release the pressure from within, and to become who you were always meant to be. The reason you were put on this Earth. Can you feel your soul calling you?

Earlier on, I spoke about the layers of your aura, and these energetic layers can indicate your ability to understand and take part in humanity evolving. Once we cleanse and clear our energetic layers, we can come to understand who we are as spiritual beings. We realise how we are able to connect to our soul and express our Higher Self to bring love, light, hope, and beauty to all of humanity and to feel unconditional love for all. That indicates our ability and willingness to surrender to the divine.

At death, our physical body dies, as well as parts of our lower aura, but our higher light bodies within our aura live on. These higher bodies contain things such as past lives and memories and our true reasons for being here, our divine spark. Once you can embrace all that you are and strengthen your energy body, you start to connect with everything contained within the aura, realising your true purpose and becoming that divine spark.

I don't expect that you would get to this place after reading through this book once. These things take time; you can, however, think of my book as a bit of a handbook, a guide, and inspiration to believe that you can transform. Maybe there are things you want to concentrate on one bit at a time and come back to other parts later.

I trust you are now aware how many different tools and techniques are available to those wishing to heal themselves. I have only touched on the possibilities. There is an infinite array of questions we can ask, methods and modalities we can use. I invite you to explore and inquire for yourself. As we are all unique, what works for some is not for others – it often takes a bit of exploration to find your groove.

Follow-Up Exercises – Self Reflection

After having read this book, how do you feel about the following questions? Maybe they will spark some intention for you to take your life, totally transform it, and turn it around. My fervent desire is that this will change the way you think and what you see is possible for you. Here are some points and ideas to consider in your journal.

- Where are you now? Go back over what you wrote in chapter one about your vision for your life. Is it still the same? Look at any statements, goals, and scales in your notes, and see where you are now and how far you have come.

- How do you FEEL after reading this? Does it trigger you in some way? Has it moved you up the map of consciousness – even if you move from apathy to anger, you have transformed and are on your way

up! I find that becoming aware and realising you can change your life often brings up strong emotions. It also means you then have a duty to yourself and can no longer stay where you are – you will either go up or down – it is your choice.

- What would you like to happen in your life? What would you like to feel? What must you have in your life? Are there things holding you back? Do you feel you can transform?

- Your elastic band will try to keep pulling you back for a while, so you need to reprogramme your subconscious – solve it in your being by facing your fears, finding where you are holding yourself back, and embracing love. This takes patience, courage, discipline, and self-compassion.

- Can you feel the love and joy that is your inner being – your inner spark of possibility, your brilliance, your confidence – calling out to you to take the bull by the horns and become that butterfly – light and free?

- Can you sense your inner flame? What ignites your inner spark?

- It is now time to live from your soul's agenda, to be able to express and experience love, truth, and gratitude. What do you feel is your soul calling?

- Can you allow yourself to flourish, for life to move through you?

- Can you find the essence of you?

- Would you like to play with life, dance with life, take things more easy?

- What steps do you need to now take to move forward? I would love to know if this has inspired you and what your plans are.

- It is time to find a passion and a focus – what will yours be? Can you find something that totally excites you, that stretches you? I am excited to think what that might be for you.

- What do you really want from your life?

- Can you list 10 passions? When my life is ideal, I am...

- Bucket list – if you knew you were going to die in one year from today, what would you do, and how would you want to be remembered?

- Perhaps you would like to find a charity or do something to help others? I have volunteered and become involved in the freedom of choice movement. I have found like-minded souls who are discerning and want a better life for their children and grandchildren. If you are interested in becoming part of a different way of living, thinking and a different medical system, separate from the existing one – one based on natural immunity, self-responsibility, prevention, and ancient wisdom – please contact me.

- Can you engage in and bring in your creative side, your intuitive side? Your fun and playful side?

Your Reason For Being

Do you now realise we are here to create, to share, to express, to love and be loved, to be inspired, and to inspire others? So stop delaying and go create – now! Complete the past, and bring forward a new way of being and living. Live your life with love and set yourself free.

We must become the very things we wish to experience in our lives, and passionate, loving feeling is the key. When we can discover these things within our being and when we can feel the love that we are and the love that we have to give, we have transformed depression into gold, and we will find our inner spark and the brilliance that shines within each and every one of us.

I have done this, and I know you can too! Good luck with everything, trust you can do this, and please reach out if you need any help or guidance.

Thank you for being here and making it all the way to the end! I am truly grateful for your time. I will leave you with this beautiful verse from Rudolf Steiner that I love to say every day with strength and conviction to build my I AM.

"Steadfastly I take my place on earth
With Certainty I walk the path of life
Strength pours into my heart
Love I carry at the core of my being
Hope I have in everything I do
Confidence in all my thinking
These six go with me through life"

Receive a Distance Healing no Matter Where You are in The World

What I love about where I am now in life is the fact that I can give distance, absent or remote healings. If you are still feeling stuck, I invite you to work with me. Have you seen the movie Avatar?

Have you seen how the seeds, trees, animals, insects, water, and leaves are all part of the web of life? Everything is alive and conscious, and interconnected. This, in reality, is how life is here on Earth, we are all connected through energy, and we all have the ability to tap into the overarching consciousness and connect with each other.

We are able to heal ourselves and others by tapping into and calling upon the divine. There are signs all around us – in nature and in our own experiences that are meant to be read and interpreted. It is just that we need to learn to recognise those signs and how to use them to create our own lives. When I utilise distance healing, I use intention to tap into the greater consciousness where I ask what you require healing with and intend that consciousness, love, all that is will heal you, show you, and provide you with what it is you need to heal.

Distance healing can be seen as a form of energy that crosses time and space to have an effect on the person receiving the healing. As such, the recipient doesn't have to be physically present to receive the healing.

As strange as it seems, this type of healing is just as effective as an in-person healing. Our own thoughts are

not interfering, we are not distracted by the physical body. My inner self is working with your physical, emotional, chemical, spiritual, soul, and mental aspects by accessing your energy body. The energy body can be accessed easily from anywhere and at any time, and that does not require you to be physically present. I do feel, however, that it does require your permission.

For most of us, our experience in this physical reality is governed by our belief that time and space are real and fixed – we believe we are separated by distance and that time only moves in one direction, forward – this is an illusion keeping us grounded in the physical world, which we need to be in to go about our daily activities and live. This illusion can sometimes limit our ability to manifest change and experience healing. It can be transcended or altered at will with practice and awareness, which is what I utilise, and thus I am able to go where there is no separation.

Recent discoveries in quantum physics now provide the scientific evidence for many of the holistic healing phenomena we have seen utilised by so many ancient societies for thousands of years.

What quantum physics has revealed in theory is that time is not fixed or linear, only flowing in one direction. Time is fluid and flows both forwards and backwards simultaneously. Your future can thus affect your life as much as your past. Your past can be altered as much as your future. From this perspective, everything is happening at once; there is no past and no future, only the present moment.

What science is also revealing about space or distance between objects is that they are actually not separate as they may seem. You and I are not actually separate but a whole. Though we might experience things as being separate from us, this, again, is merely a perception of our limited belief in the illusion that time and space are fixed.

This has been termed "quantum entanglement". This theory of "quantum entanglement" was proven with a study done in 1997 by scientists at the University of Geneva in Switzerland. Using photons of light, which is the "stuff" that our Universe is made of, the scientists revealed that two photons created by dividing a single photon into two "twins" act and behave as if they are still one and the same, or as if they had never been separated.

Therefore, if the Universe was born of the same matter, it cannot, by definition, ever be separated. In other words, it is all a hologram – the piece contains the whole, and in fact the piece is the whole and vice versa. If you are keen to learn more, then I would suggest reading The Divine Matrix by Gregg Braden.

In reality, energy does not "travel" anywhere. It is simply "sent" and "received" by intention alone and is "transmitted" instantly. It is like a waking dream state. When we alter our brainwaves to the theta state, one is able to understand, perceive, and experience a sense of the unity of all things and that there is no distance between things and no separation.

From a state of altered perception, the healer is able to then instantly access information about the client and

also instantly "transmit" healing energy to the client. From this vantage point, everything – past, future, and present – are all happening at once. All points of information are readily available, and the healer only needs to ask to see certain reference points to gain knowledge or to change events and outcomes.

I love doing distance healings because I find I get extremely accurate readings – I am less likely to be distracted by the physical body or our minds and get just as positive results as I do when someone comes to see me in person.

It's about the power of intention, the belief of the healer, and the receptivity of the receiver.

If you are stuck and unable to move, then allow me to help pull you up the ladder of consciousness, so you can begin to see for yourself where you need to go and how you can transform to find your inner spark.

References

Map of Consciousness

Source https://life-longlearner.com/how-to-measure-consciousness-using-the-map-of-consciousness-3-of-7/

11x22's Revealing & Clearing the Subconcious

Source 11x22's Mike Robinson "The True Dynamics of Relationships"
https://www.mikerobinson.eu.com/articles.aspx?aid=10

Some Great Books

Anita Moorjani "Dying to be me" and "What if this is heaven?

Jo Le-Rose "Discover your full potential"

Mike Robinson "The True Dynamics of Life" and "The True Dynamics of Relationships"

Gay Hendricks "The Big Leap"

Donald M. Epstein "The 12 Stages of Healing"

John Bradshaw "Homecoming – Reclaiming and Healing Your Inner Child"

Inna Segal "The Secret Language of Your Body"

Elizabeth Hughes "Your Body Has the Answer"

Dr David Hawkins "Power vs Force"

Greg Braden "The Divine Matrix"

Dan Millman "The Life You Were Born to Live"

Michael Mirdad "You're Not Going Crazy… You're Just Waking Up"

Evette Rose "Metaphysical Anatomy"

Dr John Demartini "The Breakthrough Experience", "Count your Blessings" and more

Napoleon Hill "Think and Grow Rich"

Eckhart Tolle "The Power of Now" and more

Rebecca Campbell "Rise Sister Rise"

Bruce Lipton "The Biology of Belief"

Viktor E Frankl "Mans Search for Meaning"

Cyndi Dale "The Subtle Body"

Tony Humphreys "The Power of Negative Thinking"

Allen Carr "Easy Way to Stop Smoking"

Tony Robbins "Awaken the Giant Within" and others

Louise Hay "You Can Heal Your Life"

Daniel Rechnitzer "Mind Lies and the Truths That Will Set You Free"

William Whitecloud "The Magicians Way"

And many more...

Movies to Get You Thinking

The Truman Show

The Matrix

Don't Look Up

What The Bleep Do We Know

The Secret

The Way

The Moses Code

The Celestine Prophecy

Leap

Pursuit of Happyness

Field of Dreams

Websites and Companies of Interest – Things I Stand for and Recommend

Australian Medical Network

Modere

Isagenix

Parents With Questions

Reignite Democracy

Esoteric Astrology Readings by Chandra

Inspirational Book Writers

The House of Brand Magic

Australian Vaccination-risks Network

IYO Club

GS Partners

Eric Davis Dental

Nutrition Diagnostics

If you would like to find out more please contact me for details

About Me

I am a wife and mother of 3, a grandmother, an author, a kinesiologist, an energy alchemist, therapist and healer, a student of life, a business woman, an investor in shares and property, an abundance coach, as well as bookkeeper for my husband's business. I have also been an accountant, bookkeeper, business manager and coach, waitress, nanny, ringer, nurses aid, cook... you name it. I am a soul, body and spirit having a human experience.

I am passionate about energy, self-development and being the best we can be, enabling us to connect in with who we really are and why we are here. I have been through severe depression, chronic fatigue, OCD, addictions, lost everything to a conman, plus a bit more. I have lived in the bush and the city and now live on the beautiful Sunshine Coast in Australia.

I understand pain and anguish and want you to realise you can transform your pain and your life and learn to love yourself – once you do that, it will transform your life. I am about love and light while being real at the same time, and I am about you being the best you can be. I am about admitting there is always more to learn.

Whilst I don't know you or why you were drawn to this book, I sense I have walked in your shoes or next to you. I have studied many modalities to become a natural therapist, so I can help people like you. In this book, I will share with

you how I transformed my depression into gold, what worked and didn't work for me, what works for my clients, and what can work for you.

My heartfelt passion is for you to escape just a little bit of the pain I and my family went through while I was ill. I want to give you the easier route to living a life of passion and brilliance. I believe we should all be responsible for ourselves and our health. I support freedom and individuality and, from my own experience, strongly oppose the road of giving in to whatever is causing us imbalance and of pharmaceuticals being the answer for everything.

I have been where you perhaps are now... in absolute despair, disconnected, unloved, depressed, beating myself up, doubting myself, feeling lost and confused, feeling guilt, worry, fear, frustration, regret, and obligation. I just didn't want to be here.

I spent my entire life never feeling good enough. Even though I came from a wonderful family, unexpected things still occurred in my life, and my internal world was never at peace.

At 18, I tried to commit suicide. I was diagnosed with severe depression and chronic fatigue in my early 30s by doctors and a psychiatrist and was told I would have to be on the highest dose of antidepressants for the rest of my life.

I never really liked myself or for that fact my entire world, and even though I met and married an amazing man and

had three beautiful children, I never appreciated what I did have.

I wasn't keen on socialising unless I was plastered. I drank every night (generally to excess) to help me numb myself and cope with the incessant noise in my head. I hid in the day if someone unknown came to the house. I was terrified of being seen for who I really was. My ego was always running the show, worried about looking successful and together on the outside while I was screaming within.

I thought that to prove my worth I had to work really hard and look after everyone else but myself. My husband and I were able to build quite an empire – I had studied accountancy, we were on the land, bought out partners, and invested in shares and real estate. We didn't have much cash flow but did have significant assets.

This still wasn't enough (as I never felt enough inside), and due to my fear of losing what we had built, we sought someone to help us, who turned out to be a conman. And we lost everything. For years we hid and didn't want to admit to family or friends what had happened. This was just further manifestation of my negative internal world. It took me a long time to realise that to find any peace I had to look at and change what was going on within. That what happened in my life was up to me. It all had to start with me.

I went to see someone and started doing courses, and my whole world started improving. I was so amazed at what was possible and decided to help others who were experiencing similar thoughts and feelings. I then realised

how many men and women experience similar thoughts and that my best chance of helping as many people as possible is to write about my experiences and what helped me.

I want you to succeed, to be happy and live your best life, to step up and own your stuff, so you can truly flourish. I trust you will enjoy my style – I come from the heart and am passionate about being able to help others. I want you to learn and experience for yourself what is possible. I am now who I have chosen to become. This is what I want for you!

With Love
Tracey

"Believe in yourself… the answers lie within, and it all starts with YOU!"

Where to from Here?

If this book has resonated with you and you would like to continue working together, please contact me as per my details below.

Get in Touch with me

www.ultimatehealing.au

https://www.facebook.com/traceyultimatehealing/

Insta - traceyultimatehealing

Email: tracey@ultimatehealing.au

Other Books by the author

Lessons from a Conman – Believe in Yourself

Qualifications/Courses/Diplomas

Degree in Bachelor of Commerce James Cook University Townsville

Diploma of Progressive Kinesiology from Your Body Has the Answer

Energy Reset Practitioner Certificate from Your Body Has the Answer

Diploma of Forensic Healing

Theta Healing I and II Practitioner Certificate

Reiki 1st and 2nd Degree and Reiki Master Certification

Certificate of Nutritional Studies

Certificate of Client Transformation from the University of Consciousness Education

Practising Member of CTAA (Complementary Therapists Accredited Association)

Golden Wings Advanced Healing Certificate

Some of the tools and Remedies used to assist in healing in conjunction with the above methods and modalities are:

Love
Sound and colour healing
Energetic light healing
Intuitive healing
Symbols
Postures
EFT (Emotional Freedom Technique)
Oracle Cards and messages
Australian Bush Flower Essences
Past Life Essences
Ultimate Healing essences and tinctures, remedies
Homoeopathic remedies
Essential Oils
Tissue Salts
Herbs
Energetic Mists
Tailored mists and remedies
Crystals
Sacred Geometry
Liquid Crystals and cards
Aura Work
Chakra Work
Acupuncture Holding Points
Inner Child Work
Archetype Work
Ancient Rekindled Wisdom Books
Scan lists and charts

Plus much more! Depends on what the client's energetic self is asking for. I look forward to working with you and am so grateful for you being here reading and utilising this book to help change not only your life but others as well.

Notes

Notes

Notes

Notes

Notes